# Building the
# Great Cathedrals

François Icher

# Building the
# Great Cathedrals

*Translated from the French by Anthony Zielonka*

Harry N. Abrams, Inc.
Publishers

# Contents

# Introduction

As the dawn of the third millennium approaches, more and more people are seeking refuge in an esoteric culture in which symbolism is often utilized for ideological purposes. The rapid development of sects represents the most visible aspect of this movement, which indiscriminately embraces a need for spirituality or mysticism and a sincere search for roots, and recruits those who are searching for an ideal that is often too systematically inspired by a past that has been reconstructed and rewritten.

The cathedrals are central to this movement. Their symbolism and significance are increasingly the subjects of debate, and they are being utilized and appropriated for purposes other than those of historical research. In addition to the scholarly studies being published by academic researchers and other undisputed experts, many publications now give competing analyses of the significance of buildings that have acquired new symbolic stature, and of the guilds of the builders who had the knowledge and skills to construct them. Studies are being published on the hidden tradition, the mysteries, and the hermeticism of the cathedrals, monuments that are portrayed as either *invisible* or in some way the products of alchemy. The same is true of the builders, who are the focus of intense philosophical disputes. They have been characterized in various ways—as the heirs of the pyramid builders, as spiritual descendants of certain Druid communities, as members of associations of initiates whose origins are lost in the distant past. A long list of detailed, thorough, and for the most part imaginary genealogies has been put forward.

*Note to the reader:* Complete information about all the illustrations in this book can be found in the "List of Illustrations" starting on page 189.

It is easy to understand the interest in the cathedrals' mysteries and symbolism. There exist, however, extensive archives of written and illustrative materials to document the true identity of the cathedrals and their builders. We now know that every city wanted a unique, special, monumental building. Each construction-site was original, and every architect had his own plan and every craftsman took his own approach to the work and utilized his particular manual and intellectual skills. From the Merovingian Age to the end of the Middle Ages, construction techniques evolved to a considerable degree, and with them evolved the way in which the construction-sites were organized and professional skills mastered. We should, therefore, be sceptical of overly generalized views of the cathedrals and their builders. The medieval construction-sites must always be differentiated in time and space.

There is no typical construction-site or any single community of builders that may be stereotyped.

*Building the Great Cathedrals* is first and foremost meant to be an homage to the workers in stone, wood, and iron who joined forces to construct a specific kind of building, the church of the bishop, which even in our own time continues to excite and stimulate diverse reactions in our imagination. With an extensive selection of illustrations and texts, this book is not intended as yet another contribution to the study of medieval construction methods. Written from the viewpoint of a historian who specializes in the study of the craftsmen's guilds of Europe, this voyage back to the time of the cathedral builders aims to shed light on the attitudes, the behavior, and the organizations of the craftsmen who built Europe's great cathedrals.

# I  THE AGE OF
# THE CATHEDRALS

# From the *Ecclesia* to the *Cathedralis*

✦ The problem of accommodating an ever-increasing number of believers (above) was one of the most crucial factors governing the decision to build larger, more spacious cathedrals (right).

✦ *Page 12:* The choir and rood screen of the cathedral of Sainte-Cécile, Albi.

✦ *Page 13:* Engineer's manual (Anonymous. India ink drawing. End of the fifteenth century).

Contrary to a widely held notion, cathedrals are not all large Gothic churches. A cathedral is first and foremost a particular church, that of the bishop, and at its center stands the *cathedra,* from the Greek name that is given to the bishop's seat or throne.

In fact, the bishop's church was at first simply referred to as the *ecclesia,* the Greek term denoting the assembly of the faithful. The bishop's house is therefore a house that receives Christians, who assemble there to pray, to listen, and to observe. The use of the term *ecclesia* became so widespread that it was applied to every place of worship. It thus became necessary to invent a new name to distinguish the bishop's church from the other churches in the diocese. That is how the bishop's *cathedra* gave birth to the *cathedralis*—the cathedral—the title and distinctive name of a place of worship around which would be assembled the services and staff of a bishop, whose powers would grow as those of the civic authorities declined.

# The First Cathedral Complexes

The age of the cathedrals predates the beginning of what we refer to as the Middle Ages. It was, in fact, during the reign of the emperor Constantine (306–337) that the Christian religion was first tolerated. In Rome, Constantine handed his palace of the Lateran over to the pope, who was looking for a suitable building, making of this first cathedral complex a space that was officially and symbolically situated within the city walls and not outside them, in contrast to the first funerary basilicas. It should be stressed that, unlike the Romans, the Christians would integrate the cult and the memory of the dead within the walls of the city by establishing the cemetery in an enclosed space; this element became an important part of a complex of buildings that was arranged around the cathedral.

In every city, the bishop and his cathedral, as well as the religious building that housed his staff, rapidly became one of the major poles, the other being the prefect and his palace. A religious, intellectual, economic, charitable, and artistic center, the cathedral complex would very soon be identified as the privileged emblem of the city.

Beside the cathedral of the earliest Christian times stood the bishop's residence, the *domus episcopi,* which housed all the bishop's associates, both religious and secular. The third major element of the cathedral complex was often a building devoted entirely to charity, a hospice or a general hospital, which was always administered by the bishop's staff.

When the state experienced its first major crises, revealing itself to be incapable of fully assuming its administrative responsibilities—a decline that continued until the eleventh century—the bishop progressively added to his religious power civic and administrative powers, which no one challenged. Quite logically, the widening of the bishop's control was also accompanied by an expansion of his territory, which was given to him by the imperial tax authorities or bought specifically to be handed over to him. The cathedral compound was thus in constant flux and represented a complex religious, administrative, and most important, architectural reality.

As the power of the secular authorities declined, the buildings symbolizing their presence and functions disappeared. Deprived of maintenance, the forums and theaters were the first victims: they were followed by the irreversible disappearance of the prefect's palace. Only the cathedral withstood the ravages of time; indeed, most were expanded in height and width. Beginning in the Carolingian period, in the eighth

◆ The cathedral district became
the hub of the city. Businesses
flourished along the main streets
leading to the church.

◆ This 1864 painting by Sir Lawrence Alma-Tadema portrays a scene that would have taken place in fifteenth-century Paris. People are leaving the cathedral of Notre-Dame by the Portal of the Virgin, after mass. The crowd of believers, which was made up of high-ranking individuals and ordinary people, was assembled inside the building within a single community, and now becomes distinct and divided as soon as they walk through the door, in accordance with their differing social ranks.

through the tenth centuries its outline was visible from a distance, and symbolizing its growing importance, it was increasingly portrayed on the stamps and seals of cities that were experiencing rebirth and expansion. In fact, from the Romanesque (eleventh and twelfth centuries) to the Gothic age (thirteenth through fifteenth centuries), the cathedral was in a constant state of evolution.

In addition to being the prime religious center, the cathedral rapidly became the focus of intense economic activity. This is especially true during the Carolingian era, mainly due to the large number of both lay and clerical people who were associated with the bishop's staff: at this time in history, the bishop had to ensure the subsistence and protection of the urban population. The cathedral was also a permanent artistic and cultural center, because of the presence of craftsmen and artists who took part in its expansion or, more simply, in its maintenance. Cathedrals attracted specialized crafts; they became sites where innovative practices and techniques were developed and where tools and equipment that were sometimes unknown to the local population were first utilized. Finally, we should note that what happened in Paris did so elsewhere: intellectual centers were generated by the cathedrals; in their shadow (and sometimes inside their walls) the earliest university teaching took place.

◆ This scene of the building of the city of Alexandria, painted by Spinello Aretino, highlights the role of the chief architect and/or the master of the works as the spokesperson for a cathedral's commissioning patrons. Work on the building site could in no case be interrupted, not even so that high-ranking visitors could be honored.

# The Gothic Age

## An Unprecedented Growth in Population

Between the eleventh and the thirteenth centuries, Europe as a whole experienced a surge of prosperity that was directly reflected in an unprecedented population explosion. It is difficult to give exact population figures for Europe during this time, but the most highly respected historians and demographers are in agreement when they estimate that between the tenth and the fifteenth centuries, Europe saw its number of inhabitants double; thus, at the beginning of the fourteenth century, the figure stood at seventy-three million people. A feeling of confidence in the future, both material and spiritual, was one of the factors that gave rise to the Gothic era.

This population boom cannot, however, be dissociated from two other phenomena that help explain the architectural explosion that the Middle Ages witnessed: technological progress in the agricultural sphere and the expansion of cities.

Until the beginning of the twelfth century,

the intensive clearing of forests considerably increased the area of land that could be cultivated. The three-year rotation of crops, the invention of the dissymmetrical plow, the new shoulder collars for horses, and more efficient tools contributed to a growth in agricultural production, which had until then been quite limited. Clearly this expansion did not affect all the regions and countries of Europe uniformly or permanently. The skills and means at the people's disposal varied greatly, depending on the landowners. It is interesting to note, however, that the Cistercian order consistently achieved some of the best harvests on its lands.

In the course of the eleventh century, cities began to experience a profound transformation. Many were born or reborn as masses of people began to flee the land, which could no longer adequately support increasing numbers of peasants. Cities were the sites of markets, of exchange, of trade, and of all kinds of meetings, and a well-organized network linking them by land and river was rapidly being established. It was the

◆ The technological progress affecting agriculture left its mark on the imagination of contemporary painters, who depicted in some detail harnesses, plows, and draft horses, the symbols of an economic renewal that favored the rapid blossoming of the Gothic style. In the middle ground are two stonecutters at work.

start of a new era—of the building of new roads, bridges, and canals, and of the control and navigation of rivers. All these projects fostered the emergence of a climate that favored innovation and new techniques.

## The Victory of Stone over Wood

Medieval society thus found itself, in the eleventh century, having to invent or redefine an architecture that could fulfill new requirements and needs. The combination of stone and wood lay at the heart of a fresh set of problems that the diverse community of builders had to confront and resolve.

In the Carolingian period, bridges were predominantly built by carpenters using wood. Gradually, stone pillars were adopted to hold up the wooden platforms, but these platforms were less and less able to cope with the ever more intense traffic. Apart from the problems linked to its maintenance, the wood used in bridges was constantly threatened by flooding. Architects looked to Roman models, which had proved successful, and began building stone bridges, incorporating openings or holes that would let water flow through whenever it rose to dangerous levels. Stone thus definitively replaced the primacy of wood in bridge construction. It was tougher and therefore more durable and more economical in spite of its higher initial cost and the need for a workforce and management that were more specialized.

The development of stone architecture in the military domain was another factor that helped assure the supplanting of wood by stone,

◆ In this miniature from the chronicles of Hainaut, the road that is being paved with stone encroaches upon the forest, whose trees have been cut down. As trade between cities increased, major traffic routes were rapidly expanded, forming an important network of arteries around the country.

◆ The city quickly became a place of political, economic, religious, and cultural power, which needed to be protected by solid ramparts made of stone.

in a trend that was still very uneven but irreversible. Feudal motes, surmounted by a wood framework tower, had long ceased being effective. Their ramparts could not withstand the burning arrows and other projectiles that were used. Here, too, stone afforded a greater degree of resistance and security. Gradually, between the ninth and the twelfth centuries, masonry took the place of carpentry, and it was backed up by unprecedented technological mastery.

In urban architecture, the same phenomenon was taking place. Within the city walls, stone facades became increasingly numerous. In addition, the old walls could no longer enclose the

rapidly expanding populations, and they had to be replaced by new ones. All the large cities were surrounded by solid and substantial fortifications expertly built of stone. Apart from the ever-present concern of protecting the city, the walls had a new function, which had as its origin the desire to bring together all the scattered enclosed spaces, thereby forming a new, cohesive entity. The stone walls thus assumed a significance that was as symbolic as it was strategic. A new community was being born, and with it there emerged a sense of urban patriotism that had not previously been imagined.

## Freiburg Cathedral

Freiburg-im-Breisgau was founded by the dukes of Zähringen in the beginning of the twelfth century. It was to become the heart of their realm, which extended from the heights of the Kaiserstuhl to the foot of the Vosges Mountains. Freiburg expanded rapidly and soon overtook the surrounding cities. Money from the mountain communities poured into Freiburg, which was a gateway to Burgundy. The little old parish church was clearly inadequate, given all that was going on in the city. The first cathedral, built under Duke Konrad, featured a nave and two side aisles, and apses in the traditional styles of Alsace and the Rhineland. Around 1200, construction began on a Romanesque church with a widely arched and vaulted ceiling, a new transept, and the towers of the roosters, which have lasted to our own time. The bays of the nave, a pure expression of the Early Gothic style, were completed by around the middle of the thirteenth century and were followed by the building of the western tower. This incomparable structure was the entirely new realization of the idea of a facade with a single tower; it was a unique and original achievement. From a brilliantly drawn plan based on an existing lower structure there arose one of the very few medieval towers that were perfectly executed. The luminous octagon of the tower, with its network of arches and pillars, and the spire, with its openwork design and network of ribs (which was completed in the middle of the fourteenth century), are truly remarkable.

—Peter Merlin, *Les Plus Belles Cathédrales*

◆ As time went by, the original walls were no longer able to contain populations that were expanding rapidly. Cities continued to grow and attract more people; like the cathedrals, cities needed more and more space.

### New Cathedrals

In medieval religious architecture, the churches were always built of stone, even though the naves were, for a long time, covered with wooden roofs. The Cistercian barns of the twelfth and thirteenth centuries provide ample evidence of this generalized use of stone for religious architecture. In the cities whose population had multiplied, bishops were eager to welcome the new faithful in larger and more beautiful cathedrals.

It is clear that the monumental dimensions of the cathedrals are closely linked to the expansion of the cities. Fulfilling a unified purpose, the cathedral towers and the civic towers together defined the skylines of cities that were more and more anxious to display their power and wealth.

## France at the Time of the Builders

Within three centuries, from 1050 to 1350, several million tons of stone were quarried in France in order to construct eighty cathedrals, five hundred large churches, and several tens of thousands of parish churches. More stone was cut in three centuries in France than in any period in the history of Egypt, even though the Great Pyramid alone has a volume of two and a half million cubic meters.

In the Middle Ages, there was a church for approximately every two hundred inhabitants; the surface area covered by religious buildings was enormous in relation to that of the cities overall. We know that in Norwich, Lincoln, and York, cities of five to ten thousand inhabitants, there were, respectively, fifty, forty-nine, and forty-one churches. Those people who had ambitions to rebuild their church over a larger area always faced serious problems: one or two neighboring churches often had to be demolished, and modern houses had to be built for the inhabitants whose homes were taken over.

—Jean Gimpel, *Les Bâtisseurs de cathédrales*

From the earliest part of the Gothic era, it was practically inconceivable to build a cathedral that was less than a hundred yards long. This desire for great size was expressed in the building's vertical measure as well. Indeed, a veritable race seemed to define the terms of the relations between cities wanting to proclaim their vitality and economic prosperity through the height of their cathedrals.

Only stone construction allowed the possibility of erecting taller and taller buildings. The legend of the Tower of Babel, which appears so often in the miniatures and other paintings of the period, testifies to this race for the sky. From one generation to the next, stonecutters and masons increased the height of the rib vaults of the cathedrals and perfected new techniques. Laon, Chartres, Beauvais, and Strasbourg all articulated the dynamics of a desire for gigantic proportions that was to spread to many parish churches, as well as to the majority of the Cistercian abbeys.

There was, of course, the problem of finding the land on which such an ambitious project could be realized. As Jean Gimpel notes, most new building required that certain existing buildings be demolished. Aside from the "old" Romanesque churches, which had often lost much of their original beauty, the areas immediately surrounding the site of the cathedral frequently had to give way to create a large building site.

This powerful movement to construct vast stone cathedrals was generated in the Kingdom of France, between Sens, Laon, and Noyon; it reached down into the southern provinces of Narbonne, Carcassonne, and Bayonne and beyond. These edifices were the most striking sign of the economic, technological, intellectual, and spiritual expansion that was spreading across Europe and was especially intense throughout the country in which it had begun, France.

◆ In England, the first cathedral in which the pointed arch was successfully developed was that of Wells (1175–1260). In the history of English Gothic architecture, this cathedral is considered a major landmark. The tracing house in Wells has survived to this day.

◆ *Pages 26–27:* The cathedral of Siena. In this Italian city, the numerous architectural "hesitations" may be explained by the fact that the entire community participated in decisions about many projects relating to the building of the new cathedral.

# The End of the Great Construction-Sites

Work on the great Gothic building sites was often interrupted mainly due to the difficulties of financing them. Building the cathedrals required enormous sums of money, which were more and more difficult to collect. As early as the first half of the thirteenth century, building sites had to close down for lack of funds. Beauvais is one of the best-known examples of the cathedrals that were not completed. Some years later, at the time of the Hundred Years' War, the defense of the city became a greater concern than enlarging the cathedral, as at Narbonne, where the city fathers refused to allow the dismantling of certain walls that were to supply stones for the unfinished cathedral. In addition to the historical reasons for these interruptions, it is interesting to observe the emergence of many legends, which gradually entered the collective memory. Parallel to the Europe of the cathedrals, there is also a Europe of legends, which offers its own, more symbolic explanation.

✦ Belgius, the founder of Beauvais and the fourteenth king of the Gauls, portrayed in a detail of a tapestry depicting the history of the kings of Gaul.

✦ *Opposite:* Masons building a palace in a detail of a fifteenth-century engraving.

## A Legend of the Knights Templars

Around Ascension Day in 1314, several mysterious horsemen stopped beside the porches of cathedrals that were under construction.

A few days after the messengers had been there, the best workers fled the building sites. Only a few disillusioned old men continued climbing onto the scaffolding, and even they had no great conviction.

Everyone was surprised to see the masons leaving their work in this way, without any apparent reason, putting their tools in their goatskin bags and going off toward unknown destinations. They were walking away in small groups; some were heading south, taking with them others they had met and corrupting the minds of those who had not received orders from the guild.

The brotherhood of "strangers" showed in this incident that it possessed a little known power. Hardly anyone dared to resist the messengers' orders. In a few weeks, the best workers in stone, wood, and stained glass had left their building sites. Almost all the cathedrals and all the other churches being built became deserted places through which the wind blew in long sighs.

—Raoul Vergez, *Les Tours inachevées*

# A German Legend

Tradition tells us that when the first outline of the cathedral of Cologne emerged from the earth, the Devil appeared to the architect, Gerhard, and threatened to stop him from completing the building by causing a canal to emerge in the middle of the foundation. Gerhard did not hesitate to wager his soul, for he alone knew the secret of how the canals were built and, because of this, was convinced that the Devil would be unable to carry out his threat.

When he went home, Gerhard is said to have told the secret to his wife, and the Devil elicited it from her by means of cunning. A short time later, when Master Gerhard saw water flowing from the foundation, he thought that he had lost his soul. He jumped down from the scaffolding into the void, and Satan pursued him in the form of a dog. The legend ends by stressing that no builder was able to finish the cathedral after that. In fact, the towers remained unfinished for centuries, until the Romantic movement turned the completion of the building into a national cause. The finished cathedral was finally consecrated in 1880, in the presence of Kaiser Wilhelm I.

# From the Cathedral Complex to the Cathedral

During the French Revolution, the cathedral complexes were not able to withstand the wave of secularization that flowed across France. The cathedrals, which had been under state supervision, became once again merely houses of worship, losing their secular role as places in which the population assembled. The cathedral complex disappeared when the bishop could no longer be housed in his palace, which was now set aside for civic or administrative purposes or, in many cases, inhabited by individuals who had no religious mission or vocation. From this point on, people spoke only of the cathedral itself, one of the key words that evokes the Middle Ages. The cathedral became a symbolic icon, one that still arouses people's imaginations. It is a place of memory, a symbolic building whose complex identity is grasped by very few of the visitors who devote to it only a few minutes of their all too precious time.

Today the cathedrals are fragile with age, attacked by pollution, and restored with the help of always insufficient funds. They nonetheless continue to attract increasingly numerous crowds, visitors for a day or true pilgrims, all of whom stand admiringly before these architectural masterpieces, these statues and stained-glass windows, fascinated by the expertise of the cathedral builders, those everyday people who dared and knew how to defy the laws of gravity and time.

◆ *Left:* View into the south transept of Strasbourg Cathedral.

◆ *Opposite:* Reims Cathedral.

beftes . 2 . Vfee fugemiv

MEEE MEEE

ŷe venim ne luy peult nuire et t t quuin laron

# II PATRONAGE, FINANCING, AND THE WORKSHOP COMMITTEE

✦ **Different Patrons in Different Countries**

✦ **The Question of Financing**

✦ **Chapters and Workshops**

# Different Patrons in Different Countries

As mentioned in the preceding chapter, a wave of great building projects swept across Europe in the twelfth and thirteenth centuries. From country to country, the identity of those commissioning and overseeing the projects differed. In Italy, with its rich and powerful trading cities, it was essentially the municipal authorities who made the decisions about the building projects, in consultation with the bishop. In England, the Plantagenets put in place a structure that was unique in Europe by assuming a direct role in the financing and administration of the construction

◆ *Below:* King Edward I, accompanied by Henri de Lacy, gives instructions to his chief architect, James de St. George, who is easily recognizable because he holds the tools that symbolize his profession— the set square and dividers.

sites. In France, the kings and princes played only a secondary role in the building of the cathedrals. Except for Saint Louis, the very Catholic king, who was responsible for the magnificent Sainte-Chapelle, in Paris, it was above all the bishops and their chapters of canons who commissioned and supervised the cathedral building-sites.

In the Kingdom of France, since the papacy of Gregory VII (1073–1085), which was marked by the desire to shield the Church from the power of the secular authorities, the recruitment of bishops was controlled directly by Rome and no longer by a few powerful sovereigns, who had until then been able to impose their candidates and were largely motivated by material rather than spiritual concerns. This recovery by the Church was accompanied by a marked strengthening of the diocesan structures. In the twelfth century, some canons in the cathedral chapters even managed to assert their authority, to such a degree that they elected the bishop and then participated in his building projects. The king or the pope was then, at least for a time, unable to impose his candidates in some vacant bishoprics, and had to be content with backing nominations over which he had no power. But relations between bishops, popes, and kings were in fact much more complex. The bishop could become a valuable ally for a king wishing to rein in contentious vassals. In the conflicts that sometimes set kings against popes, the bishops could also assume the role of conciliator, if not of arbitrator. Combined with the favorable economic context linked to the population explosion mentioned above, the political situation that favored the bishops' power also helps explain the commissioning of the great cathedrals.

Thus, in the case of France, the

master of the project was no longer the sovereign, who remained the main patron of palaces and castles. It is true that some lords and cities stand out as patrons, but in the majority of cases, bishops, priests, and canons were the true patrons or masters of the building projects. At the same time in Germany, we find the term *Bauherr,* which signifies both lord of the building and the person in charge of the building project.

## Between Pride and Necessity

Behind the commissioning of a new cathedral there was, first, a bishop who wanted to have a church that specifically represented his role and his spiritual and/or temporal power. Incontrovertibly, the abbey church of Saint-Denis, rebuilt in 1140 by Abbot Suger, sparked a desire on the part of many bishops, who were no longer satisfied with their outdated Romanesque cathedrals, for new churches executed in the Gothic style: larger, taller, and above all more beautiful and majestic. As Jean Gimpel justly writes about the bishops and archbishops who attended the inauguration of the abbey church of Saint-Denis, "they would return to their cathedrals, anxious to match this extraordinary spiritual achievement."

It is true that many Romanesque cathedrals were in poor condition, but bishops used the dilapidation and the small size of their episcopal churches to put forward a new cathedral project. In Chartres, as in Bourges, Rouen, or Nevers, fires

(whether major or minor) were also instrumental in giving some bishops and canons the idea of building a more impressive structure. The time for the Gothic style had definitely arrived.

This new art found part of its legitimacy in the very real need to accommodate an ever more numerous population of believers, a congregation that could no longer be contained in the Romanesque cathedral. But it is also true that the Gothic expansion may be partly explained by the pride of many bishops, who wanted rapidly to imitate a colleague in a neighboring diocese by planning and putting up a building that was at least as beautiful as his. There remained the problem of financing a project that had, by its very nature, to be very ambitious.

◆ *Page 32:* A stained-glass window in Reims Cathedral.

◆ *Page 33:* Model of the chapel of Rieux, presented by the chapel's principal donor, Bishop Jean Tissandier. The sculpture dates from the fourteenth century.

◆ *Left:* Saint Louis, painted by El Greco in 1590.

◆ *Pages 36–37:* The upper chapel of the Sainte-Chapelle, Paris.

◆ *Below:* Many stained-glass windows in cathedrals evoke the building sites and what daily life on them was like.

# Abbot Suger
## *and the Example of Saint-Denis*

✦ Among the scenes depicted in the stained-glass windows Abbot Suger commissioned for the abbey church of Saint-Denis are the tree of Jesse (top) and the Annunciation (above). In the latter window, the figure wearing a Benedictine monk's habit and lying prostrate at the feet of the angel and the Virgin is Suger himself.

During his administration, Suger kept reports on the rebuilding of his church, which was begun around 1135 because the main door was too narrow to admit the crowds of pilgrims. They squeezed into the existing narthex between two towers that were neither tall nor useful and were in danger of collapse. Thus masons, stonecutters, and sculptors set to work on the new narthex that was to be flanked by two tall towers.

The work that Suger had done is the best preserved of all at the abbey church. It included two bays, covered in skillfully executed rib vaults and similarly vaulted aisles. Above them was a new gallery.

By inaugurating the system of vaults with crossing ribs, Suger was able to have large bays or windows cut, through which light could flood into the vast nave. The stained-glass windows showed scenes from the Old and New Testaments, and their myriad colors glowed throughout the building. "The whole church was bathed in a marvelous even light which was let in by the most luminous windows," Suger wrote. The gems and precious stones set in large numbers in the reliquaries, chandeliers, and candelabra were also lit up magnificently.

Suger was completely overwhelmed by the enchanting nature of the house of God. "Thus," he recorded, in a famous page of his account, "when, under the charm of the beauty of the House of God, the splendor of the multicolored gems tears me away from external cares, meditation leads me to reflect on the diversity of the Holy Virtues by transposing what is material into what is immaterial. Then it seems to me that I can see myself living as if I really were in some strange region of the universe, which does not exist entirely either in the soil of the earth or in the purity of the sky. And thus, by the grace of God, I can rise from the lower to the higher realm, in an anagogic manner."

At last the church was consecrated, with great ceremony, on June 11, 1144. King Louis VII was present, with Queen Aliénor and the lords of the kingdom. Also in attendance were the archbishops of Reims, Rouen, Sens, and Canterbury and the bishops of Chartres, Soissons, Noyon, Orléans, Beauvais, Auxerre, Arras, Châlons-sur-Marne, Coutances, Evreux, Thérouanne, Meaux, and Senlis.

—Pierre Anselme Dimier, *Les Moines bâtisseurs*

♦ *Above:* The abbey church of Saint-Denis, an architectural prototype.

♦ *Left:* King Dagobert visiting the original building-site of Saint-Denis.

# The Question of Financing

The construction of a cathedral required first and foremost a very substantial financial investment in order to obtain the enormous site and meet other initial expenses. These funds would need to be added to continuously for decades. For contrary to a widely held notion, the cathedrals were not built by an army of volunteers offering their services free and compensated by their faith alone. The cathedral building-site required a vast and specialized workforce as well as a multitude of suppliers to provide the stone, wood, and iron workshops with ample quality materials. While the building sites depended unquestionably on the rhythm of the seasons, they operated primarily according to the rhythm of money. When there was a lack of it, the building site stood still for some time—a week, entire months, or even years. Many over-ambitious projects that had been definitively interrupted were simply abandoned. Financial studies for these projects had never been done because the costs were impossible to estimate, given the nature and extremely long duration of the work. The unfinished towers of the cathedrals are in themselves concrete evidence of the crucial problem of financing, which sooner or later and in the majority of cases turned out to be too onerous to bear.

◆ Paying taxes in the city of Siena, as portrayed in a painting by Benvenuto di Giovanni.

## Complex Financial Arrangements

Given the costs of keeping an enormous construction site in operation for at least a century, not to mention those of maintaining the building once it was finished, the financing of these projects had to be the product of intricate financial arrangements.

Except for the special case of Saint Louis, mentioned above, the Capetian kings played a minor role in financing cathedrals. They paid for stained-glass windows or statues representing themselves, and subsidized the cost of certain chapels. It was the bishop who, out of his own funds and the revenues of his diocese, provided the money necessary for the execution of his project. A whole category of bishops appeared who were very concerned about the profitability of their properties. They supervised closely the administration of the tithes and other financial income from their lands and properties. Each parish was asked to contribute to the building of the cathedral. Following the example of Jacques d'Amboise, some bishops did not hesitate to solemnly ask each ecclesiastical official of the diocese to offer a voluntary gift that was proportional to the revenues of his office. In Beauvais, the bishop gave up a gift of 10 percent of his annual revenues over a ten-year period, and he asked the same of the chapter's canons. But even though these sums were large, they were insufficient to cover a budget that was simply enormous. The generosity of powerful individuals was just as inadequate. In order to ensure that the building sites would open and remain in operation, it was necessary to find additional resources. Further, the bishop was unable to secure the donations and other financing and administer it himself. The chapter of canons therefore frequently got involved in financing and supervising the cathedral building-sites. Tensions sometimes arose from this dialogue between the bishop and the chapter, with the cathedral rapidly becoming a stake if not of power, then at least of influence and prestige. The vast sums of money that a chapter could control gave it, as in Chartres, unchallenged authority, which was directly reflected in the choice of people entrusted to direct and supervise the building site. The bishop has too often been considered the cathedral's only patron. In reality, the cathedral

chapter in many dioceses formed a decision-making body that was much more effective than the bishop alone; he could not, in fact, supervise or pay for anything by himself. Even if the bishop and the chapter were jointly financing the work, money still had to be found on an ongoing basis for a cathedral-building project that could quickly appear to patrons as a veritable financial abyss.

## Donations, Collections, and Relics

The appeal for donations, whether obligatory or voluntary, was addressed primarily to the powerful people of the time. In exchange for a substantial sum, the name and/or portrait of the generous donor were immortalized in a stained-glass window, sculpture, or, less visibly (and therefore of

◆ *Above:* People's relationship to money is one of the iconographic subjects treated in medieval books of morals, which were addressed primarily to the holders of fortunes that were highly coveted. In one of these works, dating from the fifteenth century, avarice is caricatured in a portrayal of a burgher who has no concerns other than to watch over and handle a pile of money, which would be very useful for noble causes, such as the building or the decoration of a cathedral.

◆ *Above and opposite, top:* Gold coins—an *écu*, a *mouton*, and a *royal*—minted during the reign of John the Good.

✦ Several corporations financed the execution of a number of the stained-glass windows in Chartres Cathedral. In addition to the satisfaction of taking part in the building of the cathedral, these generous donors were able, in this way, to display the greatness of their trade for all time and to proclaim their economic success. The stained-glass window of the Redemption (above), made in the thirteenth century, was financed by the blacksmiths, who are shown at work. The window of the Apostles (opposite) was executed thanks to the donations of the bakers.

# The Milanese Model

In order to avoid an excessive quantity of gifts in kind (animals, pieces of cloth, jewelry, small change from many places), the council of the Milan Cathedral workshops regularly organized auctions. The city's bankers, who were entrusted with the financial management of the workshops, were thus able to convert into monetary units all the goods, furniture, and property that had been donated, with a view to ensuring that the building would actually get built.

The major expense of salaries alone (almost 40 percent of the total expenditure) required a continuous cashflow, as workers were generally paid on a weekly basis. To this sum it was usually necessary to add the cost of supplies and transportation.

The technique of double-entry bookkeeping (credits and debits), which was mastered by the Milanese bankers, was undoubtedly a considerable advantage that contributed to the success of the building project. This type of rigorous and methodical bookkeeping was soon imitated and widely adopted.

—Philippe Braunstein,
"Grands Chantiers et hommes de l'art"

◆ Italy: a laboratory in the practice of bookkeeping.

less interest to potential donors), in a book specially prepared for the occasion.

All over Europe, associations were formed to assist in financing the work on the cathedral. Founded and placed under the patronage of a saint, these associations welcomed well-off clergymen and lay people, such as bishops, canons, prominent civic dignitaries. They were asked to pay a contribution to join and an annual membership fee. Most sums collected in this way went directly into the coffers of the cathedral workshops. Following the example of Troyes, some cathedrals benefited from the financial support of several associations, which coexisted in the same city and whose sole purpose was to cover the costs of the building. This type of society should not, however, be confused with the guilds and other associations of craftsmen, which were also associated with paying for the cathedral but at a different level. In Chartres, among other places, for example, the guilds donated stained-glass windows.

Collection boxes or chests set up all around the city, not only in churches, provided another means of soliciting donations. In Autun, for example, some were placed in a draper's or goldsmith's store, appealing to individuals in both sacred and profane places and at different moments throughout their daily lives. Christians felt proud and honored to make their small contributions to the building of a structure that, though it belonged to the Church, was the house of all believers. Of course, things were different when the urban and rural populations were pressured too intensely. But, in spite of their undeniable importance, the funds collected through the collection boxes represented only a fraction of the construction budget.

Some donations were in kind; they included horses, mules, donkeys, oxen, as well as jewelry and medals; those managing the project

◆ *Opposite:* The expansion of the medieval construction-sites was matched by an increase in the minting of money.

would sell these items for coins, which were much more reliable and easier to handle. Nevertheless, the generous spirit of the common and poor people, as well as the more self-interested contributions of powerful individuals, remained quite insufficient considering the huge scale of the expenses that had to be covered.

Bequests and willed legacies were strongly encouraged and solicited. The mendicant orders, which had been the great beneficiaries of this practice, now found themselves engaged in intense competition with the cathedrals, which enjoyed a privileged position in the imaginations of those who knew they were soon to die. Declaring that one wanted to bequeath one's land and one's wealth (or even part of it) to contribute to the work

✦ Reliquary crucifix of
Pope Urban V, said to contain
a piece of the veil stained with
the blood of Christ, offered by
Pope Urban II to the emperor
Charles IV. The crucifix
belongs to the collection
of the cathedral of Saint
Vitus, Prague.

on the cathedral meant that one was assured of being remembered in masses and prayers (which was so important for the salvation of the soul) that would be said in this place. The poor and the most destitute were thus the true losers in the great wave of offerings and various kinds of gifts that were now being diverted from strictly charitable purposes to the bishop's church, the church of the whole city. And yet, ever newer and better resources had to be found to reach out to the whole of the Christian people: the time for large-scale collections and the displaying of relics had come.

Popes Honorius III and Urban IV granted indulgences to those people who would finance the building of the cathedrals in Reims, Clermont-Ferrand, Bourges, and Narbonne. Collections were organized throughout the entire kingdom from those among the faithful who wanted to obtain forgiveness for sins that they had committed or would yet commit. These practices would form the basis of Martin Luther's criticism and

## The Case of Strasbourg

Until the thirteenth century, it was the bishop who bore the main cost of the financing. In Strasbourg, there are letters of indulgence, which were sources of financing the building of the cathedral until about 1275. We do not know of any instruction given by the chapter of the cathedral to the workshops, as was usually the case in the building of all other cathedrals. The voluntary contributions of the cathedral clergy and the bishop, which were recorded in the register of donors, were far from sufficient. From the third decade of the thirteenth century, the cathedral's funds began to increase dramatically, and by the end of the thirteenth century, it was the burghers of the city who were providing all the financing.

—Barbara Schock-Werner,
"Le Chantier de la cathédrale de Strasbourg"

condemnation of the Catholic Church in the early sixteenth century.

The great innovation was indisputably the organizing of collections in association with the displaying of relics. This was a practice that had, of course, been known and utilized before, but it now assumed dimensions that had not previously been imagined. *Questores,* holding authorizations from the bishop, traveled throughout the diocese asking for money and exhibiting the relics of martyrs and saints, while proclaiming the virtues, merits, and beauty of the building that was to be constructed. Above all, they stressed the importance of the salvation of the soul, which was much more important to people at the time than aesthetic concerns are to people today. But these traveling displays also posed a number of problems. Some bishops took offense at the movement through their diocese of relics that belonged to another one. Restrictions were therefore put into place, and territorial boundaries were sometimes

necessary in order to avoid disputes concerning exclusive access to donations. Swindlers also took part in the movement; disguised as clergymen, they showed false relics. They were not, of course, the only ones to use this stratagem, but they did collect donations that would never be paid into the cathedral coffers.

The collectors solicited anyone and everyone. Thus, thieves and receivers of stolen goods were promised absolution and forgiveness on condition that they give up all or part of the goods that they held illegally not to their rightful owners but to the Church, which would make good use of them. Lords, princes, kings, and queens were attracted by very famous relics. Often cited in this regard is the case of Cologne Cathedral, which owed a large portion of its financing to the relics of the Three Wise Men. These attracted many powerful individuals from all over Europe, who visited the sanctuary and left behind alms and donations that befitted their rank.

✦ *Above:* The display of relics of the saints (here, Saint Nicholas) occasioned grand ceremonies at which the Christian people's imagination and piety were channeled toward financial goals.

✦ *Pages 48–49:* Stained-glass windows were an essential element of the cathedral in many ways, one of which is that they served as paintings that depict particular moments in the building's history, from its construction to its consecration. The history of the cathedral is intertwined with that of its patron saints, who were often the models for architects. These builders sought to attain an eternal glory, provided by the stained glass and its luminous colors, that would radiate through the ages.

# Chapters and Workshops

Once the first sums of money had been collected, what was needed, above all, was a way of managing the finances. That role was assumed by the workshop committee, the organization that was entrusted with the direction of the cathedral project. The workshop committee was not made up, as is often claimed, of all the canons of the chapter. Rather, it would elect one of its number to supervise the efficient running of the project. In many cases, the chapter appointed a lay person to this very important office. The representative of the workshop committee should not be confused with the architect of the cathedral. This misunderstanding, which still occurs today, is based on the vocabulary that was used at the time. In fact, the representative of the workshop was given titles that could lead to some doubt as to his true function. In several ecclesiastical texts, he is called the *operarius* (worker), *magister fabricae* (master of the workshop), or even *magister operis* (master of the works). It was very often this man who was entrusted with finding the architect, the technical expert who was capable of transferring the project chosen by the workshop committee into a concrete reality that would be clearly visible to people who, having been intensely solicited to support

the project, were now waiting to see the fruits of the financial sacrifices they had made.

It was no longer possible for the master of the works or the patron also to function as the architect or master builder. In the tenth and eleventh centuries, when the absence of true professionals in architecture made itself acutely felt, clergymen, bishops, or abbots had very often been obliged to act as masters of the works. During this period, an essential role was played by the Cistercians, whose competence and professionalism in the architectural domain helped build their reputation. The Gothic cathedral project necessarily presupposed a project director or master builder capable of responding to the vision of the chief architect, who had produced a plan that was impressive in its enormity. He would give the plan shape in drawings and models and, above all, would translate it into a full-size reality.

The workshop committee thus took care of the administration and financial management of the cathedral project, and when it allowed itself to be guided by enlightened experts, it could also ensure the architectural continuity of the building over time, throughout the fashions and styles of successive periods. But to begin with, the chapter and the workshop had to find an architect, a task that was as difficult as overseeing the finances. An intense competition began.

✦ *Above:* Seal of the Oeuvre Notre-Dame, Strasbourg.

✦ *Opposite:* Abbey church of Pontigny (Yonne).

## The Administration of the Finances at the Strasbourg Cathedral Site

The master of the works' job was to record accurately the income and expenditures associated with the building of the cathedral and to ensure the safekeeping of the title deeds. He also had to manage the upkeep of all the buildings of the Oeuvre Notre-Dame, guarantee the payment of salaries, distribute donations fairly, and make available sufficient quantities of all the necessary materials. He did not have a specific budget but was, in fact, the director of the budget for the entire project.

Donations and bequests destined for the building of the cathedral were the fundamental reason why the workshop committee was created as an autonomous legal and financial institution. The authority of this body was considerably enhanced in the course of the centuries and enabled it to have permanent direction of building projects independent of vicissitudes, disruptions, or famines.

—Barbara Schock-Werner, "Le Chantier de la cathédrale de Strasbourg"

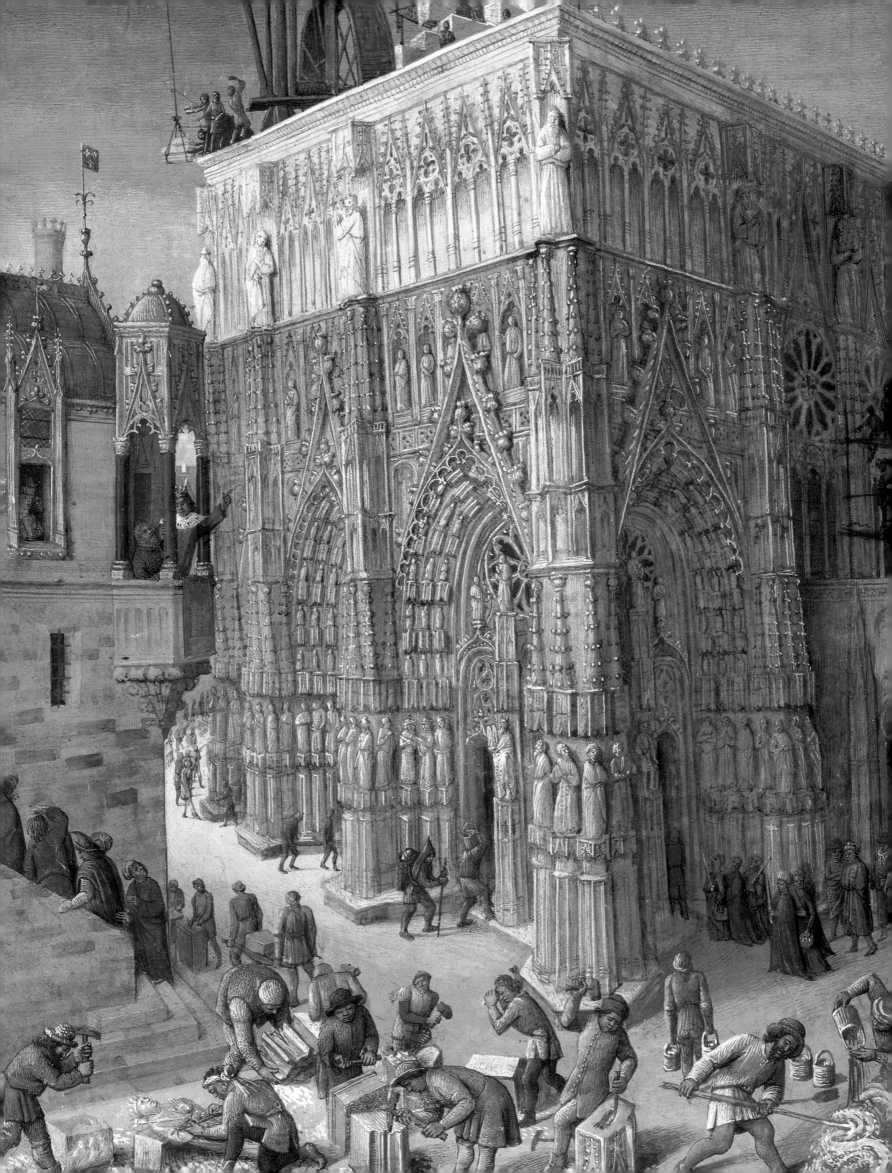

# III  THE ARCHITECT

# Obtaining the Commission

◆ *Page 52:* A fifteenth-century miniature by Jean Fouquet depicting the building of the Temple of Jerusalem.

◆ *Page 53:* Detail of a figure from a miniature illustrating the construction of the cathedral of Aachen.

The selection of the architect of a Gothic cathedral was no simple task. It was the result of a choice made by the master of the works and usually the chapter and its dean, who after solemnly interviewing several applicants nominated the one who had managed to win their confidence, as much with his abilities and the solid training he had received in the field as with the appropriateness of what he had said and of the drawings or models he had presented. The chosen candidate was also the one who had managed to hold the attention of a chapter that had both a precise and a vague idea of the nature of the building it wanted constructed. The

chapter knew very little about the financial, human, material, and technical feats that they would be able to realize on a project whose completion date could not be predicted with any certainty.

Drawings, however interesting they might be, were not terribly useful in allowing the architect to make people understand and appreciate his plan. The decision-makers' imagination had to be fired by presenting something more concrete and easy to comprehend, since the clergymen of the chapter and/or the lay people on the workshop committee were not all experts in the art of geometry.

The project was therefore presented with the help of small wooden, wax, plaster, or papier-mâché models. Some of the models are themselves finished works of art of outstanding quality, such as the one that was presented to illustrate Our Lady of Ratisbon. Far from being approximate, the models were to be the exact representation of a scaled-down version of the building that would become more and more precise with time. The value of the models was not limited to the stage of choosing the architect. They could later be used to explain to all the workers on the project exactly what was expected of them. But in conceiving and designing a great monument made of stone, the models clearly would not suffice. What was needed were plans, sketches, and working drawings.

## A Privileged Position

The architect was closely linked to the patron or master of the works, who appointed him. His first mission can be summarized in a very obvious statement: to search for and to find solutions

◆ *Left:* A very fine model of the church of Our Lady of Ratisbon, made entirely of wood, to illustrate the project of the architect Hieber.

◆ *Opposite:* The architect was also, and above all, the person who knew how to draw and trace.

that would fulfill the aims of the project for which he was recruited. As Alain Erlande-Brandenburg rightly stresses: "His genius is unfurled on the day he meets the patron or master of the works, who forces him to solidify his ideas and give them form. Architecture is born from this duality: a master of the works/project director and an architect."

But the architect was not just a worker appointed or chosen as a result of the experience he had acquired in the field working on one building site after another. He was not only, as people too often assume, the person who could realize a plan that may have been drawn up by others. As an intellectual with solid training behind him, an expert in the art of building, the cathedral architect enjoyed an authority and status that up until that time was reserved for lords and rulers. To be convinced of this observation, we need only look at the many pictorial representations that show him on the cathedral building-site as the equal of the patron or master of the works. Right beside the king, holding his scepter, stands the architect, with his set square and dividers, the honorary attributes of his occupation.

# *When an Architect Dies*

Ulrich of Ensingen died on February 10, 1419. But the premature death of the master (the work he had planned had not been completed) did not bring the building site in Strasbourg to a halt. It does seem, however, that at the time the Oeuvre Notre-Dame must have experienced some difficulty in nominating his successor.

In the summer of 1419, the architects Maternen of Frankfurt-am-Main; Jergen of Württemberg, the architect of the cathedral of Freiburg-im-Breisgau; and Erhardt Kindelin of Sélestat arrived in Strasbourg. All three were invited by the Oeuvre Notre-Dame to give their opinions on the state of the project and how it should be continued. The committee paid for the cost of their trip and offered them a meal on a platform that stood up on the scaffolding.

Based upon the advice that they gave, the Oeuvre Notre-Dame entrusted Master Jean Hütz of Cologne with the direction of the construction project in Strasbourg, thereby rejecting Master Ulrich's own son, Matthew of Ensingen, who would leave Strasbourg for Basel, taking with him his father's plans and projects, an act for which he would be severely reproached.

—Michel Zehnacker, *La Cathédrale de Strasbourg*

A man of knowledge, the architect was also a man of power. His privileged position on the building site and in society at times caused intense jealousy. All the legendary and mythical texts transmitted within and by the builders' associations illustrating the murder of an architect convey this message, even if their main function was to emphasize the necessity of passing skills on to others. If this did not happen, a building site would have to be closed down whenever the chief architect died. It was in this spirit that the workshop committee had, above all, to embody the spirit and direction of the project, to ensure the continuity and ongoing vitality of the cathedral buiding-site if the architect died or went away, either voluntarily or having been dismissed by a dissatisfied patron. We should note in passing that in most cases the plans drawn up by or under the authority of the architect or master of the works did not belong to him. They had to be returned to the workshop committee, which remained the sole authorized guardian of the project.

## A Letter of Appointment

The bishop, dean, and chapter of Meaux send greetings in God to all who will read this letter.

We hereby announce that we have placed Master Gautier de Varinfroy, from the diocese of Meaux, in charge of the construction project of our church, subject to the following conditions:

He will receive ten livres every year, for as long as we ourselves, our successors, and the said chapter shall allow him to work on the said site. In the event that he should fall ill for long and continuous periods of time, so that he can no longer work, he would not receive the said ten livres.

He shall also receive three sous a day while working on the building site, or when he is sent to do work in connection with the project. In addition, he will not be able to accept any work outside the diocese without our permission. Further, he will receive the wood from the building site that cannot be used there. He will not be allowed to go to the building site at Evreux or to any other site outside Meaux, or to remain there for longer than two months, without the permission of the chapter of Meaux.

He will be required to live in the city of Meaux and he has sworn that he will work faithfully on the above-named construction site and will remain loyal to that site.

—Letter of appointment of Gautier de Varinfroy,
future architect at the cathedral of Meaux, October 1253

### Detailed Contracts

From the moment he was chosen by the chapter, the architect found himself tied to the master of the works by a contract that specified, in detail, the rights but also the duties of both parties. Placed under divine auspices, the contract sanctified their relations, which it was hoped would be as harmonious and loyal as possible.

Prospective architects usually had to make the honorary commitment not to work on any other building site within the diocese or outside it. The fear of seeing an architect dissipating his energies by working simultaneously on several sites was omnipresent in the contracts of appointment. In return for his exclusive engagement he would be richly compensated: the chapter would finance his salary and often even supply him with clothing that befitted his increasingly important status.

◆ The contract hiring architect Hans Hammer, drawn up in 1486 for the building site of Notre-Dame in Strasbourg.

# A Man of Many Skills

The chief architect of a Gothic cathedral played several roles while pursuing a single vocation. An architect or engineer, he was also the general manager of the building site and was not above getting down to work with his own hands when the circumstances required it. Unlike many architects today, the medieval architect was thus not a pure intellectual, who left the job of constructing his cathedral to the manual laborers. The intellectual/physical dichotomy did not exist on the cathedral building-site. Everyone there shared a perception that the work of the mind was also the work of the hands. The architect was like his craftsmen: he thought about what he made and he made (or tried to make) what he thought of.

If he were a former stonecutter, the architect could reserve for himself the execution of the most delicate or most visible sculptures. He did not hesitate to request the help of colleagues who were able to make contributions to the aesthetic success of his project. Similarly, the architect who had previously been a carpenter could take part in assembling a particularly difficult or decorative wooden framework. Journeymen and architects (still the current name of a craft-guild journal in France) thus belonged to the same community of craftsmen, a community that had its hierarchy but was also a brotherhood, whose leader could choose to blend in with his companions, provisionally giving up his status as an expert and becoming one worker among

◆ *Above:* Detail of a drawing executed in the fourteenth century for the facade of the cathedral of Strasbourg.

◆ *Pages 60–61:* Painting of 1845 by Théophile Schuler portraying the building of Notre-Dame in Strasbourg.

many others once again. This aspect is often overlooked in the histories that have been written on cathedral building-sites, including the pictorial representations of them that have come down to us.

## Sketches, Plans, and Working Drawings

In spite of the high cost of parchment, drawings helped make a project more specific for the chief architect and for the master of the works. The facade, the side elevations, the chapels, and the spires were all the subjects of drawings that were supposed to depict clearly the architect's ideas. The building that housed the Oeuvre Notre-Dame, in Strasbourg (see chapter VI), to this day contains one of the finest and most important collections of drawings on parchment, the oldest of which date to the thirteenth century.

A privileged spokesperson in relations with the cathedral chapter, the architect was also,

✦ At Chartres, some of the stained-glass windows (that of Saint Chéron, especially) are extremely informative, enabling us to better appreciate the labors of the stone-cutters and other artists who worked on the cathedral building-site and in the lodge.

and above all, a senior craftsman who had to assign and explain jobs to the different participants on the cathedral building-site. He could rely on his own experience as well as on the help of specialists, whose role has too often been overshadowed by that of the architect.

Working drawings, which were so important for the stonecutters, for example, explained schematically how the stones were to be cut and positioned, an art that would later be called stereonomy. Different techniques are illustrated at Reims, Narbonne, Soissons, Clermont-Ferrand, as well as at Roslyn, in Scotland, and Byland, in North Yorkshire: how to cut the stones, the equipment to be used, as well as notes on details to be included. In Rouen, Strasbourg, Paris, Wells, and York, there were famous tracing houses in which the architect and his assistants could have full-scale working drawings executed, using set squares and dividers. The drawing area of the York tracing house was seven by four yards, allowing full-size

drawings to be produced. Unlike the engravings rendered directly on stone, most of the drawings made in the tracing houses disappeared when the buildings were completed.

## Templates

In the famous stained-glass window of Saint Chéron, in the cathedral of Notre-Dame in Chartres, we can see several wooden templates. Also known by the name of "moles" (which could also refer to drawings), they were used to draw architectural sculpted members—such as the outline of a base, rib, or mullion—and were usually painted different colors.

The templates were not made by the architect but by older or retired craftsmen, who wanted to preserve a record of an art and techniques that had been perfected over the course of long years of labor on the building sites. In each lodge, the templates were preserved with care.

# The Architect and His Workers

In thirteenth-century Europe, the tradition of travel was already firmly in place. But it was not enough simply to find an architect to construct the desired building. It was also necessary to recruit workers to carry out the plans. The example of Etienne de Bonneuil, who traveled to Uppsala, Sweden, with ten journeymen and apprentices, is a good illustration of the way Gothic building techniques were spread by architects, highly skilled technicians, and journeymen, who because of their skills and their reputations were called to distant building sites. The architect traveled with his team of equipment makers, stonecutters, and carpenters, craftsmen he knew because he had worked with them or trained at the same time as they had in the building trades.

Two centuries after Bernard the Elder (Santiago de Compostela), the names of individuals like Etienne de Bonneuil (Uppsala), Matthew of Arras (Prague), and William of Sens (Canterbury), among others, continued to make widely known a French school that was highly appreciated for the quality of its architectural knowledge and skills. But the movement was not simply

✦ This fifteenth-century miniature illustrates a ceremony of solemn thanksgiving for the building workers organized by the Hospitalers after the Siege of Rhodes. In this detail, workers wear colored bands around their heads and carry with them the symbolic tools of the earliest craftsmen's guilds.

directed from southern Europe to the North, and France did not have an exclusive monopoly on skills. In 1483, the Alsatian architect Niesenberger was invited to go to Milan to raise the dome of the city's cathedral. The master did not go there alone: thirteen workers from different countries went with him.

A sound knowledge of architecture depended on the craftsmen's traveling to new and faraway building sites to encounter different techniques, methods, and people. In our own time, the journeymen of the Tour de France continue to respect the same principle, which states that progress in the acquisition of knowledge necessarily takes place through travel. The French style, which during the Renaissance would come to be known as the Gothic style, thus owed its development to the departure of many Frenchmen for more and more distant horizons. The famous miniature painting depicting a ceremony held after the Siege of Rhodes, in 1480, illustrates how the crafts were organized in a network that extended to the edges of Europe, under the influence of architects and craftsmen who had come predominantly from France.

The Kingdom of France was not, however, only an exporter of talents that were in high demand. It also welcomed skilled craftsmen from abroad. The cathedral of Reims was built, in part, with the collaboration of journeymen stonecutters from Germany. The cathedral building-sites were thus true crossroads of different crafts and skills, and of people from many regions and countries. In this respect, the Tower of Babel is a perfect symbolic representation of a building site, on which several languages were spoken. This helps explain

◆ In this miniature, which appears in the *Recueil sommaire des croniques françoys,* the architect who presided over the building of the cathedral of Aachen is shown bearing the features of Charlemagne.

## The Architect of Reims, Hugues Libergier

The tombstone of Hugues Libergier, the architect of Saint-Nicaise, in Reims, who died in 1263 and was given the great honor of being buried inside the building, illustrates remarkably well the high social standing and privileged status that was enjoyed by a cathedral's architect.

> *Here lies Master Hugues Libergier*
> *Who began working for God on this church*
> *In the year of Our Lord 1229*
> *On Easter Monday and who died*
> *In the year of Our Lord 1263*
> *On the Saturday after Easter*
> *Pray for him.*

Depicted on an engraved stone, the architect stands under an arch holding a model of the building. He is dressed in a long robe and hooded cloak, and wears a hat that resembles those worn by doctors. Is every architect not, in fact, a doctor in stone, a *doctor lathomorum*?

The measuring rod, the set square, and the dividers are the symbols of his profession.

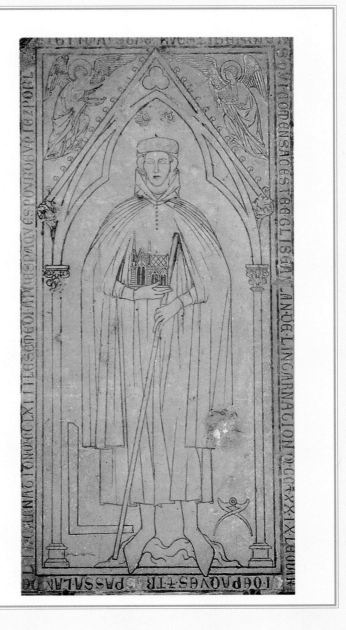

why there was a desire, on the building site, to establish distinctive signs that did not require the use of a language that all of the workers did not necessarily speak. A headband, a color, knee-length stockings for apprentices: an entire system was gradually put in place, and it was prominently featured in paintings of scenes at the building sites. The legends of the craftsmen's guilds that place the mythical origins of these associations at the time of the building of the Temple of Jerusalem merely transfer, to an Orient that fired people's imaginations, the organizational structure that was emerging on the cathedral building-

sites. It was a structure that required a clearly defined hierarchy and an order that was universally recognized and respected. The chief architect (James, Soubise, and, much later, Hiram), the patron or master of the works (Solomon), and the cathedral (the Temple of Jerusalem) all saw their common mission sanctified by this transfer to an Eastern context: they were all participating in work that celebrated the glory of God. Jean Fouquet's painting is the most famous example illustrating this phenomenon, since the Gothic cathedral in that scene is supposed to be a representation of the Temple of Jerusalem.

# IV BEFORE REACHING THE CATHEDRAL CONSTRUCTION-SITE

# The Quarry

## "The Search for the Quarry"

On construction projects in the Middle Ages, the same difficulty had to be faced as does today—that of having available a supply of quality materials in a location that is close to the building site. Apart from the search for solid timber and well-tempered metals, finding the desired quality and supply of stone was, in fact, one of the first priorities of both the builders and the project's financiers.

Beginning in the eleventh century, when the large-scale building sites began operating, finding a quarry was the primary preoccupation of both the patron, whether king, lord, bishop, or abbot, and the master of the works. They wanted to locate one that was not yet being exploited and that would not, therefore, have to be bought out. It also had to be quite close to the construction site, in order that transportation costs could be kept to a minimum.

The quarry had to meet three essential criteria: easy access, high-quality stone, and proximity to the building site. Patrons and their emissaries searched for both new quarries and, more frequently, old deposits that were no longer being exploited. Indeed, the accounts of many of the workshop committees show a budgetary line for "the search for the quarry." For example, an entry in the account book of the cathedral of Autun for the year 1294 reads, "For research into the condition of the Marmontain quarry, one livre and ten sous."

The ideal was obviously to have suitable stone available on the spot, in the immediate vicinity of the building being erected. All that had to be done then was to extract the stone and cut it. But the bounty of nature has its limits. Even if local quarrying was very helpful for the building

♦ *Page 66:* Wood and stone, two materials that were essential for the construction of large buildings, had to be hauled by road and by waterway.

♦ *Page 67:* Construction begins on the great church of Bern in 1420.

♦ *Right:* In this sixteenth-century ink drawing describing the construction of the monastery of Schönau, the work performed by the quarriers and the carters is not forgotten.

of military sites (the Cathar castles in the Aude region of southern France were the prime example), this convenience was much less apparent when the authorities were trying to find stone that was suited to more grandiose ambitions. A cathedral was not like a castle or simple defense construction; it required a very special type of material, of sufficient quality and in ample quantities to meet the expectations of the patron and architect and the needs of the project.

There was always the possibility of demolishing a building or taking stones from an existing monument, as in the case of Beauvais, where the walls of the city were utilized for this purpose. But in most instances, this solution was inadequate. The decision had to be made either to start up a new quarry or to rent or buy an existing one.

## A Miracle of God

The Lord Bishop Gerard realized that among the obstacles that might delay the project that was so dear to his heart, none was more difficult to overcome than the slow transportation of columns that had been cut far from the city. He therefore prayed to Almighty God to grant him a quarry that was not so far away.

Having gone riding one day, he explored the hidden depths of the earth in many surrounding areas. Finally, with the help of God, who never disappoints those who place their trust in Him, he had a trench dug in the village that had always been called Lesdain, which was four miles outside the city, and he found stone there out of which columns could be cut. That was not the only place: by having people dig even nearer to the city, on the property of Nigella, he had the joy of finding quality stones of a different type. Thanking God for this discovery, he devoted all his zeal to his pious project.

—Anonymous, published in V. Mortet and P. Deschamps,
*Receuil de textes relatifs à l'histoire de l'architecture*

✦ A sculptor at work: detail of a miniature in a fifteenth-century edition of Pliny's *Natural History.*

## Cartage

Transporting stone was very costly. When the quarry was distant, a combination of transportation by road and river often had to be devised. Enormous quantities of material had to be moved from the quarry to the port, loaded onto and unloaded from the barges, and transported to the building site itself. The sums for all of this rose rapidly. There were also numerous tolls to pay along the way, even though the chapter attempted to persuade lords and princes to allow free passage in exchange for prayers and masses or even a promise of burial in a sacred space—an abbey or monastery, if not in the cathedral itself. Such favors were helpful to the salvation of one's soul.

Although it is impossible to establish reliable statistics

✦ At the cathedral of Laon, an homage to the oxen, whose labors were indispensable.

✦ *Opposite:* A fifteenth-century miniature by Jean Colombe depicting King Priam rebuilding Troy, from the *Recueil des histoires de Troie.*

on this subject, it may be noted that from the purchase price of the stone at the quarry to the price charged upon its arrival at the construction site, it was common to see a fivefold increase, which was the case at the cathedral of Troyes. According to Pierre du Colombier, one pair of oxen could barely transport a single load of fifteen hundred kilograms per day over an average distance of fifteen kilometers round-trip. With the development of modern harnessing in the ninth century, horses could at last be used. By causing the weight to be borne by the horse's neck, ancient harnessing compressed the horses' chests and made it difficult for them to breathe, exhausting them very rapidly. By shifting the weight onto their shoulders and by introducing shoulder collars, as well as nailed-on horseshoes, modern harnessing facilitated the animals' movement and endurance. But if horses were faster, oxen were still used more often because of their greater strength. Sometimes powerful harnesses were used. One chronicle reports that the master of the Conques building site had his legs broken by a cart drawn by twenty-six pairs of oxen, which were transporting capitals from the quarry to the church. (By sculpting the capitals at the quarry, a significant weight was cut from the overall load and costs were reduced.)

Furthermore, if the countryside separating the quarry from the city was even slightly hilly, cartage costs increased: the teams of oxen had to be changed frequently in order to guarantee the minimum number of deliveries that would keep the building site supplied with material.

More docile and stronger than horses, oxen made a mark on the memory of some architects, such as the one at Laon, who insisted on paying homage to them by having sixteen oxen depicted in stone at the top of the building, on which they, too, had labored.

◆ This miniature shows stone-cutters at the quarry and masons on the building site. Stone that had been rough-hewn on site was lighter, therefore less expensive to transport. However, if the stone-cutters were working at the quarry they needed templates and precise models. In addition, they had to be provided with board and lodging. The financial incentives were great for finding a high quality quarry near the cathedral building-site and the city.

## Open Quarries and Mines

As noted above, the master masons' understandable desire to lighten by as much as possible the volume of stone to be transported meant that the stone was first worked on in the quarry itself. There blocks were chiseled down and preliminary cutting was carried out. Stone was extracted either in the open or in mine galleries. The cost varied considerably, depending on the method utilized. Mining was more expensive because carpenters had to be employed to shore up the galleries to avoid cave-ins. This was one more group of men and materials for which financing had to be found.

Good quarrymen were rare. Apart from the dangers of the job, they needed above all to have gained a thorough knowledge of the subject to be able to detect the layers of stone, to estimate their height and value, and to calculate the best possible way in which to cut blocks of stone. Stone was extracted using basic tools—pickaxes, crowbars, and wooden wedges. Armed with these implements and knowledge that was passed from one generation to the next, the quarryman was the first participant in the process of building a cathedral. It was he who supplied other workers, who were equipped with different tools, with the blocks of stone that they would shape into columns, capitals, or stones that the skilled hands of the craftsmen would sculpt and cut into images of enduring beauty.

## The Quarrymen, the Unknown Workers

There were great disparities between quarries, as far as the workers who labored in them were concerned. In some cases, as at Troyes in the thirteenth century, it was the workers who had been hired for the cathedral building-site who went to the quarry to rough-hew and cut down to size the stones that they would see again in the city, after the inevitable cartage and/or transporting by barge. Much more frequently, however, when the quarry belonged to an owner who had his own workers, it was they who did the cutting down to size and the rough shaping of the blocks.

Armed with wooden wedges and mallets, the quarrymen cut enormous blocks from the

✦ In this illustration depicting the construction of the great church of Bern in 1420, the blocks of stone have already been rough-hewn before being transported to the building site. Here they are being raised by means of a claw. At the workers' feet are the principal tools of the stonecutters and quarriers, including sledgehammers, dividers, and rulers. Pictured above is a stonecutter's pickax, and below is a crowbar.

rock. Gradually, the stones emerged from the bottom of the quarry. Ropes were fastened around them, and with the help of winches and pulleys or of wheels, blocks weighing up to eleven hundred pounds were hoisted out. The blocks were immediately cut down to size by stonecutters, who gave each stone its definitive dimensions with the help of the templates discussed above. Contracts stipulated the measurements that were required. In the absence of an equipment technician who could be sent to the quarry to supervise and assist the quarrymen, it was the working drawings, patterns, and other sketches that outlined what was needed.

In order to bring the rough-hewn or cut stones to the carts that would transport them to the city, two systems of transportation worked side by side in the quarry over a period of many years. For a very long time, wooden stretchers carried by two workers were the only means of moving the stones. The invention of the wheelbarrow, which is mentioned as early as the thirteenth century,

allowed for a considerable reduction in the workforce. Both methods were used on the cathedral building-site, since it was not enough to load stones onto the carts; they also had to be unloaded at the end of the journey.

The term "quarryman" deserves some explanation. It denotes, first and foremost, the person who extracted from the quarry the thousands of cubic yards of stone that were necessary for the construction of the building. The quarryman (or quarrier) was often ignored by those who drew up the inventory of the builders of the cathedral, but he should be given a place that befits the importance of the work he did. As is revealed by Etienne Boileau, who does not mention them in his *Livre des métiers* (Book of professions) the quarryman did not benefit from the glory that was systematically accorded to every stonecutter. Scarcely any better paid than the simple laborer, the quarryman sacrificed his youth and health in the quarries. Exposed to the vagaries of the weather in the open

◆ A marble quarry in Carrara, Italy.

mines, or threatened by silicosis in the under-ground galleries, he was often considered one of the common people if by some misfortune he did not know how to cut stone. Not accustomed to moving from city to city, he was excluded from the stonecutters' guilds, at least from those that made travel their main distinguishing feature.

The term "quarryman" can mean the un-skilled laborer, the foreman, or the master of the quarry; these occupations were very distinct from one another and were remunerated and taxed quite differently. As a general rule, based on the studies of British scholars, including D. Knoop and J. P. Jones, the quarrymen worked in groups of eight. Each group was placed under the author-ity of a master quarryman, who was sometimes known as the chief quarryman, and who enjoyed a salary that was 50 percent higher than that of his quarrymen. But the term "master quarryman" refers much more commonly to the owner of the quarry or to the person who oversaw its operation, if it had been rented. An owner and entrepreneur, the master quarryman had practically nothing in common with the ordinary quarrier or even the chief quarryman. The amounts of money he re-ceived were, at times, colossal, reaching a hundred times the salary of a quarryman. This figure may be explained by the fact that many master quarry-men were paid for each of the stones they ex-tracted from the quarry. In the accounts of the Autun workshop committee, the quarryman, Mas-ter Chevillard, was paid in direct relation to the number and size of stones he extracted.

✦ The great cathedrals required high-quality stones that could withstand the effects of time. Here, Chartres.

◆ A forest in Alsace.

# The Forest

In the Middle Ages, wood was a ubiquitous material in Europe. However, uncontrolled deforestation, which affected western Europe in the eleventh and twelfth centuries, at times made the rare types of wood that were sought out for building (most notably, oak and chestnut) very difficult to obtain. Moreover, cities were using up more and more wood for construction, heating, and the craft industries. By the eleventh century, there were few cities that could still obtain from their environs all the trees they needed. This was not the case in the building of abbeys in rich rural areas surrounded by forests. La Chaise-Dieu is typical of these huge forests, from which abbeys cut oaks, ash trees, and willows at much lesser cost by taking them only when and as the building processes dictated.

Aristocrats anxious to preserve their hunting grounds were opposed to the increasing clearing of forests and to the creation of open spaces in them. The forests thus became the battleground between those who traded in wood, those who wanted to graze their herds in them, and those who saw them only as hunting grounds. But under the influence of the king and certain monastic orders, such as the Cistercians, the conflicts would gradually give way to a much more coherent and rational approach to an environment whose many and diverse resources were claimed by several different groups.

Building timber requires straight and very long tree trunks, which can only be found in mature forests. Few fine tree trunks came from the areas near cities. In contrast to the quarries, patrons of cathedral projects generally did own forests that contained the wood necessary for the construction, but they were often judged to be too distant. The problem of transportation thus usually involved costs that were foreseen and described in detail in the workshops' accounts. Although wood was much easier to transport than stone, the cost of moving it was still quite high, and patrons were always anxious to obtain supplies of timber from forests as nearby as possible.

In the age of the great cathedrals, mature standing timber was therefore the object of special concern. Among the lords, cities, bishops, and workshop committees there was a movement away from the anarchy that had marked the use of the forests to a more rational system. The Order of Cîteaux played an important role in this change, as it developed the first sawmills powered by water mills. Furthermore, in their desire to extend their lands, the Cistercians initiated innovative management techniques and operating methods. When timber was cut down on demand, the squared-off tree trunks were stored in the Cistercians' barns until the master carpenters arrived. They would order and pay for the wood, and have it transported to the building site.

On the cathedral construction-site, it was imperative that the minimum quantities of wood needed be secured. For in spite of the victory of stone, wood remained an indispensable material, in building stone arches, the wooden framework of the roof, and for scaffolding. As already mentioned, it also played an important role in propping up mining galleries in the quarries.

# Timber for Saint-Denis

In order to find the beams, we consulted those who work with wood in our own region, as well as in Paris, and they told us that, in their opinion, we would not be able to find any beams in these regions, because of the lack of forests. They said that we would have to get them from the region of Auxerre instead. They were all in agreement on that subject. But, for our part, we were overwhelmed by the idea of so much more work and by the great delay that it would mean for the project. One night after returning from matins, I began to think, as I lay in bed, that I should myself go around the nearby woods and look everywhere to try and limit the delay and all the extra work by finding the beams myself. I therefore put aside all other concerns and set off early in the morning with some carpenters and the dimensions of the beams, and I traveled quickly to the forest of Rambouillet. Passing through the valley of Chevreuse, I called together our seargents, those who looked after our lands, and all those who knew the forests well, and I asked them to state under oath whether we had any

chance of finding beams of that size in that area. They began to smile and certainly would have burst out laughing if they could have, professing their astonishment at our ignorance of the fact that no such beams could be found in this whole region, especially as Milon, the lord of Chevreuse, who was our liegeman and one of two people who held half of the forest from us, and who had for a long time waged war with the king and Amaury de Montfort, had left nothing intact or in a good state, having himself built three-storied defensive towers. We chose to reject all that these men said to us and with bold confidence we set out to explore the whole forest. After about an hour, we found a beam of the right dimensions. What more did we need? By nones, or a little earlier, pushing our way through the thick forest of tall trees and thornbushes, to the astonishment of all those who were present around us, we found twelve beams. It was the number that we needed. We had them carried joyfully to the holy basilica and placed on the roof of the new building, to the praise and glory of the Lord Jesus, who had reserved them for himself, as well as for his martyrs, wishing to protect them from the hands of robbers.

—Abbot Suger, *De Consecratione*

✦ *Above:* A carpenter's adze.

✦ *Left:* Woodcutters at work in a detail from a sixteenth-century miniature.

## The Cathedral Is a Forest . . .

These vaults that are chiseled to look like foliage, these jambs that support the walls and stop abruptly like broken tree trunks, the coolness of the vaults, the darkness of the sanctuary, the dark wings, everything in Gothic churches recalls the labyrinth of the forests; everything makes one feel the religious awe, the mysteries of God. . . . The Christian architect was not content to build forests; he also wanted to build their murmurs and, by means of the organ and the hanging bronze that he attached to the Gothic temple, even the noise of the winds and of the thunder that rolls in the heart of the woods.

—Chateaubriand, *The Genius of Christianity*

◆ *Opposite:* In the background of this fifteenth-century painting the artist has shown the basic process by which scaffolding was assembled.

◆ *Below:* Building an abbey in the time of Charlemagne, as imagined in about 1460.

The building of a cathedral often made it necessary to clear large areas of forest. As Abbot Suger's text makes clear, this role was given to the carpenters, who went to the forest to cut the timber needed to build the workshops, the scaffolding, the lifting equipment, the many arches and other moldings, and the most important and noble work, the wooden framework of the roof.

The carpenters did not operate alone; assisted by laborers and sometimes by the chief architect or master of the works, they sawed and cut up large quantities of trees—3,944 trees for Windsor Castle alone, in the middle of the fourteenth century. The accounts of the workshop committees always highlight this corps of carpenters and their laborers, who were employed to cut down and transport the timber. For example, in the account book of the workshops of Amiens Cathedral, we read: "For the cutting and transportation of timber destined for the arches of the church of Saint-Lazare, for the carpenters and laborers: seventeen livres, two sous, seven deniers."

The carpenters were not the only people involved in the search for timber; mention should also be made of everyone who took part in the work of getting the timber out of the forests: tree splitters, dockers, chasers of animals, sledgers, ox drivers, cart operators, and boatmen—all the various specialists and their apprentices who are generally left off the list of those who worked on the cathedrals.

◆ The forge at the abbey church
of Fontenay.

# From the Forge to the Workshop

In the study of the cathedral building-sites, there is also an erroneous tendency to see the utilization of the forest as having been limited to the needs of carpentry. However, the forests also contained the principal supply of firewood and were therefore very important to the workshops and factories that depended on wood and charcoal. Forges, glassworks, and brickworks were set up near forests to be close to this prized raw material. Transportation costs, a recurring concern, according to the account books and financiers, were thereby limited.

Metal was of course used by Gothic architects as well. It was primarily employed to make the iron bars and chains used in vaults and arches. It also required a suitable place in which to be worked and prepared. Spain is often cited as having supplied a number of building sites at quite a high cost, showing that metal was imported for this purpose. But we should not ignore the existence of mineral ore deposits in many of the countries and regions in which cathedrals were being erected. The places where the metal was smelted from ore were very seldom located near the building site. The Cistercians always gave special importance to the search for metal ores and to their use, going so far as to place the forge inside the abbey, as was the case in Fontenay. But as a general rule, forges were usually located near forests or deposits of ore.

Stone quarries, forests, and sand quarries were not the only places that were involved in the work of the building site. Mention should also be made of distant workshops such as those of the casters, who made the bells that were so longingly awaited and so highly esteemed when they rang out at the cathedral's consecration. Tile kilns were set up in the very heart of the forests (such as the forest of Mauny, for Rouen Cathedral) before they were moved to the cities, near their ports, the true centers of the cathedral-building enterprise. Some cities specialized in producing soda and cobalt oxide (substances that went into the making of glass), coal, lime, lead, tin, and iron, while others, such as Montpellier, supplied raw materials that came directly from the East, via the Mediterranean.

We must therefore dismiss the idea that the cathedral building-site operated independently. The need for black marble, slate, alabaster, copper, lead, tin, plaster, and other materials required that most of the workshops form part of a highly organized commercial network. Major as well as minor rivers played an essential part in the transportation of supplies to the construction site. The places linked to the building site were thus numerous and varied, nearby and distant, but they served a vital function in the progress of the building project, ensuring a constant supply of raw materials and ready-made items to architects and masters of the works, who paid very close attention to these matters.

◆ A blacksmith at work, from a fifteenth-century woodcut.

# V  THE CATHEDRAL CONSTRUCTION-SITE

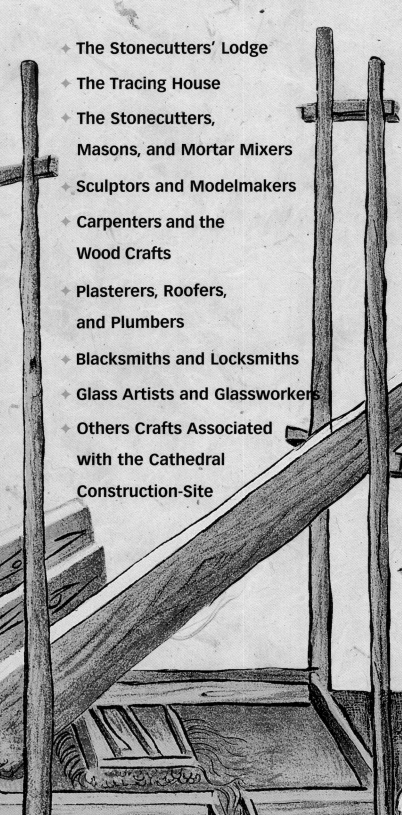

# The Stonecutters' Lodge

## A Place of Work, a Community

Whether it was called a *Hütte, lutza, cassina,* or *loge,* the lodge appeared on almost every building site in medieval Europe. This building was generally built right up against the cathedral or a few yards away from it, of wood or stone, and it served several functions, material, social, and symbolic.

The lodge was primarily a place of work, a site where tools were arranged and stored, a privileged space in which orders were given, and a welcome shelter from bad weather, having the considerable advantage of being heated in winter. Whenever the building site was closed for any length of time because of icy or other inclement conditions, the lodge became a training center where the master and craftsmen taught their art to the youngest workers, the apprentices. However, contrary to a widely held notion, the stonecutters did not live in the lodge, even though some of them could stay there when they wanted to take a short rest.

With regard to the occupancy of a lodge, there seems to be agreement that the average number of members was at the very most twenty, including apprentices. Most of the time, the lodge was dissolved upon completion of the building work, or after the death of the master in charge of it. If the building had not been completed, the new master created a new lodge, and he was not obliged to keep the members who had been chosen by his predecessor. This was, of course, the case for the cathedral building-sites that employed several generations of stonecutters and architects. Naturally, from one site to another and from one lodge to another, there were exchanges and customs, but these traditions were not organized or codified into a comprehensive or hierarchical system. It was not until the fourteenth and fifteenth centuries that the first official attempts were made to group together lodges and to regulate their statutes, as happened in Ratisbon.

A large number of paintings and miniatures, especially those from the fifteenth century, show the lodge as open, with its interior visible, whereas in reality it was very often a site that was kept hidden from the eyes of the public. Closed off by wooden panels or stone walls and sometimes simply covered with leather skins, the lodge was above all a special place in which the techniques and the secrets of the crafts were passed on. Such training was not to be given where anyone might see and hear it, and the lodge was therefore a protected place; gradually, it would assume a sacred character.

✦ *Page 84:* The cathedral construction-site, a place of intense activity, as this modern illustration suggests.

✦ *Page 85:* Detail of a drawing depicting daily life for builders in the fifteenth century.

✦ *Left:* The depictions of mythical building sites (here, the Tower of Babel) regularly pay special attention to the lodge, which is shown here as a place of work.

## From Independent Lodges to the Grand Lodges

The organization of lodges differed according to country. It is therefore appropriate to speak not of the lodge at the time of the cathedrals but of lodges, so varied were the systems and statutes from one country to another. The *Regius* (1390) and *Cooke* (1425) manuscripts evoke the organization of masons and stonecutters in England; also of interest are the important Statutes of Ratisbon (1459), which relate to the stonecutters who had come from all over Germany to unify their respective sets of rules. These statutes were revised and updated in 1563 under the generic title of the Statutes of Saint Michael and were better known as the Orders of the Grand Lodge of Strasbourg (see chapter VI). Although these documents should not be assumed to apply to a single organization that existed throughout Europe, they do reveal a highly hierarchical system in which several fundamental values were solemnly proclaimed: fraternity, honesty, preserving trade secrets, faithfulness to one's oath, professional and moral duties at all levels of the craft, professional training, and, of course, prayer.

## Different Organizations in Space and Time

France does not seem to have had the kind of organized system that Germany or England did. Only the Duty of the Tour of France, later to be called *le compagnonnage* (the association of craftsmen's guilds), outlined, at the very end of the Middle Ages, an attempt to form an organization based on travel and mutual support, although its size and identity could not compare with those of the English or German associations. The emergence and the structuring of French guilds were not, however, contemporary with the building of the first Gothic cathedrals, even if these cathedrals undoubtedly provided the foundations for the Compagnons du Tour de France (Companions of the Tour of France). The absence of reliable documents does not allow us to deepen our understanding of the French system, and it unfortunately remains quite mysterious by comparison with the other countries mentioned.

✦ *Above:* This engraving after a drawing by Albrecht Dürer shows a lodge that is open to the outside world.

✦ *Below:* The Four Crowned Men, patrons of the crafts of stonecutting and laying. From the *Regius* Manuscript.

◆ The hall of the lodge that may be seen in the Museum of the Oeuvre Notre-Dame in Strasbourg. It was built by Hans Thoman Uhlberger between 1579 and 1582.

◆ Pages 90–91: The interior of Chartres Cathedral.

Rather than the lodges of modern Freemasonry, which have borrowed the symbols and vocabulary of the crafts of masonry and stonecutting (which they do not practice), it is the current chambers and *cayennes* (community meeting-places) of the Companions of the Tour of France that appear to be the true successors of those builders' lodges, because their primary function is the transmittal of techniques and knowledge within a professional brotherhood. It is nonetheless true that, in contemporary Masonic imagery, the term "lodge" and the manuscripts and other medieval statutes regulating the organization of masons and stonecutters are sanctified or utilized for clearly symbolic rather than historical purposes.

The *Regius* and the Statutes of Ratisbon must be read in their entirety in order that we may understand fully the memory of a realm of builders that is too frequently reduced to a single model, which is supposed to have existed wherever cathedrals were being built in Europe. The real picture is much more complex and difficult to describe.

The type of organization evoked by the Statutes of Ratisbon is especially interesting because they originated in the everyday experience of those who toiled on the building sites. In fact, the system defined in Ratisbon was deeply inspired by that of the lodge that existed in Strasbourg in the thirteenth century, when the cathedral's nave was under construction. Thus, the Statutes of Ratisbon remain one of the primary documents on which to base a description of the functioning of a lodge at this time.

## Everyday Life in the Lodge

Three major titles, which were already in use before the statutes were written, were recognized and used in the lodge: master, companion, and apprentice. At the level of vocabulary, there was nothing very different here from the system used by the corporations, but as far as the lodge's functioning and internal rules were concerned, this was a completely different system. A master was nominated to be the head of each lodge; he would apply the statutes and see to it that the members respected all the customs. A man of power, the master was, first and foremost, a man of knowledge who, in contrast to the corporations, had the duty to teach his art without charging any fees: "No craftsman or master shall require that a companion give him any money in order that he show or teach him anything to do with masonry. In the same way, no supervisor or companion may show or teach anyone anything in sculpture in exchange for payment" (Orders of Strasbourg).

Similarly, in contrast to the corporations, the apprentices received wages (*gages,* as in *engager* and *désengager,* to hire and to fire, respectively), meals, and upkeep from the lodge. However, a system of security payments seemed to be standard practice, so that the young men would remain for the full term of their apprenticeship, which lasted for five or even seven years.

The lodge was very precisely organized. The master had his reserved place at the east end of the meeting room, and no one else could occupy his spot.

The working day was regulated by the ringing of the lodge bell. Work was carried out from daybreak until sunset. Some English regulations, dating from 1370, indicate a one-hour break for lunch and a drink break of a quarter of an hour in the afternoon. In summer, two breaks of thirty minutes each were allowed. During the "bad months," the lodge let go almost half the workers because the laying of stones was stopped due to the risks of ice and frost; in such cases, the columns that had already begun to be built were covered up with straw and dung. Those who did not have work at the lodge went to the quarry or, more

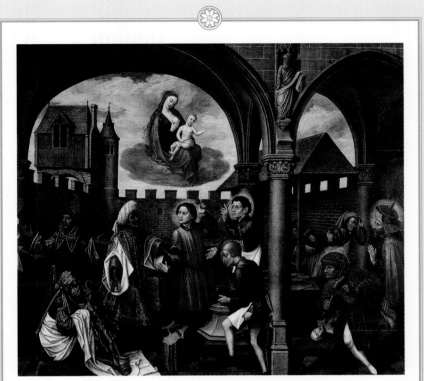

✦ Detail of a sixteenth-century triptych portraying the Four Crowned Men.

## *The Four Crowned Men*

Legends situate the Four Crowned Men in the third century A.D., in the reign of the emperor Diocletian. These four stonecutters were called Claudius, Castorius, Symphonarius, and Nicostratus, though their names vary in the different versions of the legend; Sévère, Severian, Carpophorus, and Victorian often take the place of the names just cited. Having converted to Christianity, they refused to make, for Diocletian, a statue of the god Aesculapius. The legend specifies that the four stonecutters were locked alive inside lead coffins and thrown into a river. Other texts place them inside lead-lined barrels, which were thrown into the sea. Whichever version is the true, the four stonecutters who had sacrificed their lives in order to remain loyal to their faith were elevated to the rank of saint and given the title of the Four Crowned Men. Pope Melchiades is said to have decided that they should be honored on November 8 of every year.

In the associations of stonecutters, masons, roofers, and other brotherhoods across Europe, the Four Crowned Men were considered patron saints. This is still the case today. The tradition was particularly esteemed in Italy and throughout the area influenced by the former German Empire. Thus, from the early Middle Ages, the *ars quatuor coronatorum,* the Art of the Four Crowned Men, specifically designated the arts of stonecutting and masonry.

♦ Certain manuscripts from the fifteenth century, such as this one illuminated by Jean de Courcy, portray the master of the works in full symbolic dress. The military fraternity of the master of the works and the craftsmens' fraternity of the architect represented two complementary, rather than opposite, worlds.

frequently, returned to the land they cultivated in winter. Almost everywhere, there was a summer salary and a winter salary, the latter only two-thirds of the former. It was forbidden to work on Sunday, the day of the Lord. In England, people also rested on Saturday afternoon. There were also the days on which no work was done (forty, on average, in the year). The stonecutters especially honored the Four Crowned Men, who were venerated as the patron saints of their corporation.

## A Hierarchical Brotherhood

The community was gradually transformed into a professional brotherhood. The Statutes of Ratisbon, and later, the Orders of Strasbourg make explicit in several articles the rules that should preside over the admission of apprentices, companions, and masters. Signs of recognition, meant for the members of the brotherhood of workers in stone, were also established. Far from assuming a secret or esoteric character, which some of our contemporaries see in them, these signs indicated one's membership in a community of peers, who recognize one another as experts in a particular profession. They were often masons' marks.

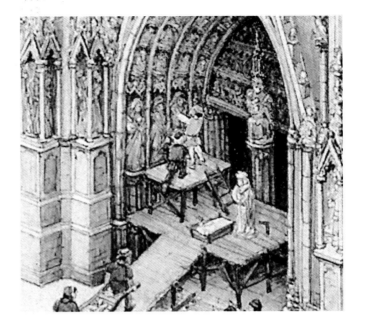

An apprenticeship was fixed at five years. Afterwards, the apprentice could be admitted to a lodge as a companion and further trained. He nevertheless had the possibility of leaving the lodge to travel and work at another construction site.

Immediately below the rank of master of the lodge was the *parlier* (speaker), a Germanized form of the French term *parleur,* that is, the person who would transmit the master's advice and explain or translate plans that were sometimes very complex. In France, especially, the equipment manager seems to have assumed the role of the speaker. The term "supervisor," which is found in the statutes of 1563, illustrates the move

toward a much more hierarchical type of organization, one that was concerned to check or supervise the quality of the work done and the respecting of orders that had been given. The statutes established in Ratisbon thus marked the end of an era, one in which each lodge had been fully autonomous and independent, having its own jurisdiction and regulations.

In the front rank of the professions represented on the building site, those considered the "high professions" were primarily the ones organized around a lodge, a word that would rapidly become widely used to denote not just a place or building but the community itself. The age of the great cathedrals heralded the age of the great lodges.

◆ *Above and opposite right:* These details from contemporary drawings by Philippe Fix show the various communities of craftsmen who worked on the cathedral building-site.

◆ *Page 94:* A thirteenth-century mosaic in the basilica of San Marco, Venice.

✦ The memory of stones: marks, signs, signatures, and other symbols visible in the crypt of the cathedral of Verdun.

# Masons' Marks

*Five types of masons' marks may be distinguished:*

### ✦ The Pieceworker's Mark

The stonecutter was paid by the piece. He thus had to put his personal mark on each stone that he worked on, so that the master stonecutter could verify the completion and the quality of the work and could pay the cutter accordingly. As a general rule, the pieceworkers' marks were geometrical in shape and extremely simple.

### ✦ The Positioning Mark

These marks should not be confused with the pieceworkers' signatures. Generally made up of small engraved squares, crosses, or arrows indicating the direction in which the stones were to be placed, they were incised on the inner face of the stones and were therefore difficult to see.

### ✦ The Mark of Provenance

Some buildings include stones that have on one of their faces (generally the one that was incorporated into the stonework) marks that have no other purpose than to indicate the geographic origin of the stone. These marks enabled the different quarries to be distinguished, and thus paid, and they allowed laborers to arrange the stones on the building site according to where they had come from.

### ✦ The Master's Mark

Given to the sculptor or stonecutter by his peers, this mason's mark enabled the most important pieces of the whole building project to be signed. It was nontransferable and valid for the duration of a stonecutter's life. Most of these marks, as at Strasbourg, for example, are variations on the numeral 4 (Four Crowned Men, Four Grand Lodges of the Empire). The study by Franz Rziha proves that all these marks reflect a logical order that is complex but coherent, and based on an old order incorporating the four major lodges of the Holy Roman Empire.

### ✦ The Sign of Honor

This mark was given to a companion stonecutter. It was transformed into a crest and became a genuine coat of arms, which was incised on stones.

# The Tracing House

There is some confusion surrounding the name given to the specific space reserved for the making of drawings, sketches, and plans relating to the construction of the cathedral. This confusion is in part linked to the fact that depending on the building site, the drawings were executed either in the lodge (which was the case on most building sites in France) or in a tracing house, a separate, small building that was distinct from the builders' lodge. In Milan, for example, the work-

◆ A drawing on the paving stones in the cathedral of Bourges.

shop committee placed the drawing house on the second floor of a shed adjacent to the lodge. Drawings could also be made in the open air. But the confusion of places, lodge or tracing house, was largely caused by the confusion of words, since drawings, working drawings, sketches, blueprints, outlines, and plans represented quite distinct entities, which could not be described by a single term. Since the nineteenth century, there has been a strong tendency to combine these different techniques and to see them as part of a single family, and to use the word "drawing" to mean something other than what it actually did.

For example, there are many texts and anecdotes that describe the use of plans of abbeys, churches, or cathedrals that had been traced directly into leveled ground. The story of Pope Liberius tracing the plan of Santa Maria Maggiore in the snow that had miraculously fallen encourages us to imagine that a cathedral could first be drawn on the ground itself. Some documents confirm that this practice did exist, such as the account book of the abbey of Vale-Royal, where in 1278 there is a reference to the payment made to a group of workers who were asked to level the ground in order that a plan of the monastery could be drawn. This custom is now recognized by many historians and other specialists, who are in agreement that plans were originally worked on, full-scale, on the ground itself. However, these plans should not be confused with others, such as those of the cathedrals of Narbonne, Limoges, or Clermont-Ferrand, where only a detail or portion of the building was traced onto the paving stones at the construction site for the workers to follow. But as a general rule, these plans were most often drawn in another part of the building site, after a bed of plaster or clay had been laid down. The cost of parchment was extremely high until the fourteenth century and prevented excessive use of this material, even though it could be easily transported. Working on a surface of soil, sand, clay, or plaster, one could start over again and again, add corrections at once, and make additions day by day, none of which was possible with parchment, which also always had to be quite small in size.

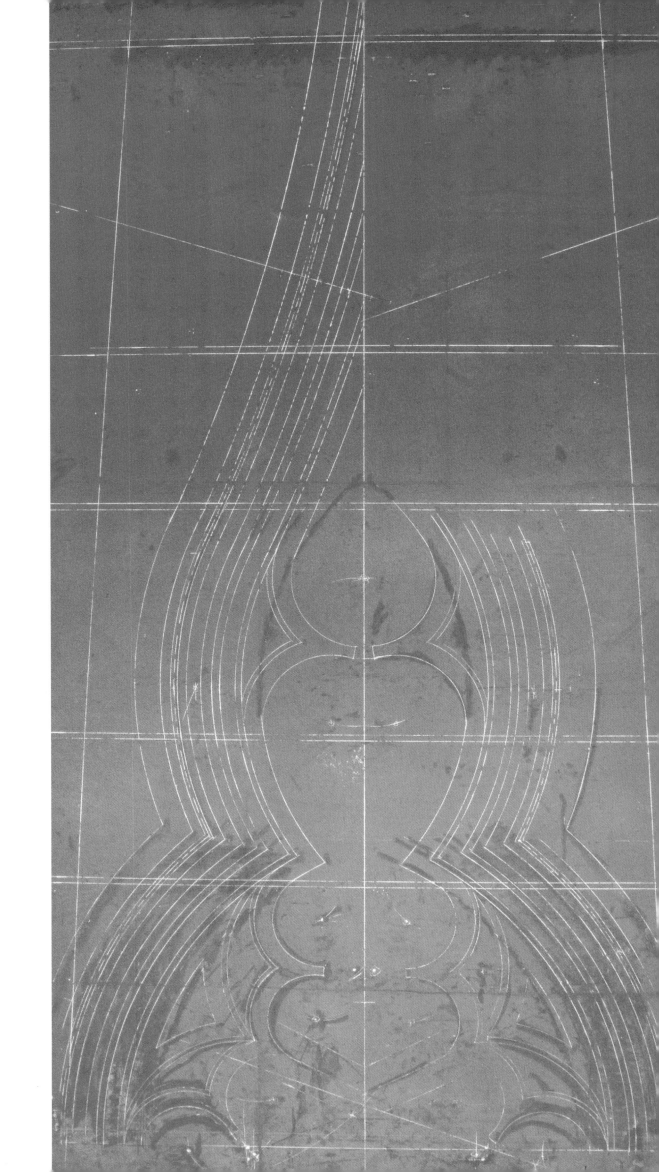

◆ An architect's working drawing on tracing paper.

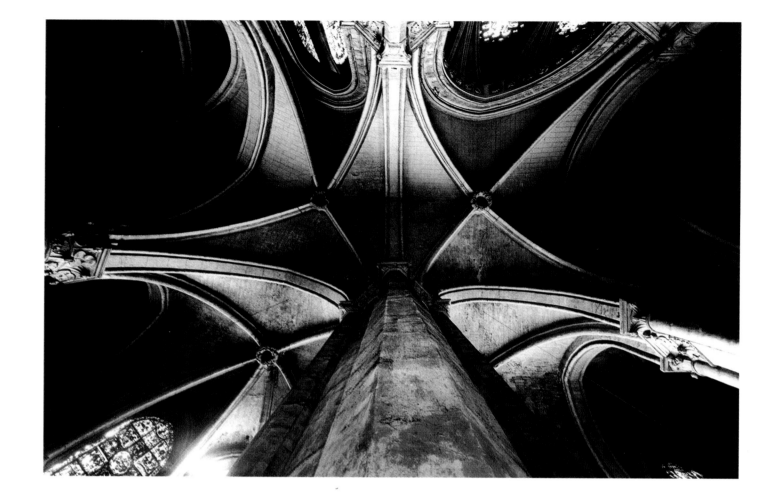

◆ Vaults in the southern ambulatory at Chartres. From the initial working-drawing to the reality of the completed building, the builders' entire wealth of knowledge is made concrete here.

More than just plans, these drawings, which we still see engraved on the paving stones of some cathedrals, express a kind of descriptive geometry, which lives on today in the heritage of the Compagnons of the Tour de France under the general term *trait* (line or drawing).

Apart from those mentioned above, some drawings were made on pieces of parchment that were often affixed to each other to form a larger sheet. They represented either the whole building or a part of it. This practice seems to have been employed especially in the Germanic countries. Pierre du Colombier speaks of it when discussing the cathedrals of Vienna, Strasbourg, Prague, Freiburg, Ulm, Esslingen, and Ratisbon. The primary function of these drawings was to provide comparative documentation, since the plans of Notre-Dame, in Paris and Orléans, also appear on parchments that have been found in a number of German cathedrals. The drawings could thus serve as starting points for an architect. We can be more certain that before any building or rebuild-

ing project was begun, the drawings were presented to the chapter, the bishop, or other patron to give them a clear idea of what the building would look like and to define it in relation to existing buildings.

In England at the beginning of the fourteenth century, tracing houses are mentioned in which the architect and his assistants not only made drawings but also prepared sketches or patterns for cutting the stones. Elsewhere a *trasura* is mentioned. But here, we are going beyond the narrow framework of the simple drawing to a more complex technique, whose main objective was to prepare smaller-scale projections, which the workers would later enlarge. This technique, which was highly esteemed by the masons and stonecutters, was also practiced by the carpenters. Today's Companions of the Tour of France have continued the practice. This is the very heart of the secrets of the profession; how the builders went from the plan to the actual building is a subject of ongoing debate.

✦ In the Gothic era, Vitruvius's treatise on architecture, dating from the first century, was still a major reference work for many architects. For the cathedral of Milan, for example, the architects drew plans of great complexity to realize their grand visions. In the background, a sixteenth-century engraving shows a cross-section of the Milan cathedral. The three photographs show different views of the cathedral today.

# The Stonecutters, Masons, and Mortar Mixers

In the medieval family of stoneworkers, a distinction was often made between two essential functions (and therefore two distinct types of training). In twelfth-century texts, the term *lathomus* is given to the person who cuts the stone, giving it its shape. By contrast, *cementarius* refers to the person who laid the stones, attaching them to others with cement or mortar. Here, too, terms vary depending on geography and time. For example, in his famous *Livre des métiers* (Book of the professions) of 1268, the provost of Paris, Etienne Boileau, described in a single chapter, without making any real distinctions between the terms he was using, the "masons, stonecutters, and mortarers," the latter term specifying to some extent the work done by the *cementarius*.

## The Mortar Mixer

Learning the craft of the mortar mixer or mortar maker was, for some workers, a specific stage in the professional development of those who wanted to work with stone. Far from being the job of a laborer, which does not assume any particular knowledge, wielding the trowel that produced the mortar was an essential task that to a large extent determined the quality and longevity of the building, since the mixture prepared was used to cement the stones together, to cover the walls, and to coat the vaults. The term "trowel" is still found among the terms employed by the French craftsmen's guilds to designate a specific responsibility. Badly prepared or badly mixed mortar could represent a real danger, both to the workers and to the building they were constructing.

The mortar mixer was the person who knew how to mix water, lime, and sand, which were brought to him by his young assistants. A few troughs, buckets, or tubs and shovels were usually enough for the stirring of the mortar, which must have been made very close to the building site. The mortar mixer ordered the mixture and decided on the best form of transport, either on the workers' backs, in tubs, or on stretchers, with a single concern in view: to make certain that the quicklime had not set by the time it reached the site. Mortar mixing was an art that did not suffer amateurism or improvisation.

The job of the mortar mixer was neither menial labor nor noble craft. The mortar mixer thus enjoyed much greater respect than that received by the mere carriers of water, stone, and lime. These men were laborers, often recruited locally, who were paid by the piece or by the day.

A proof of the special role of the mortar mixer was the many representations of him in manuscript illuminations and paintings relating to Gothic architecture, even though, in fact, these more often showed the apprentice than the master mortar mixer and layer. There was a tradition of mortar mixing and the number of "mortar-mixing" streets in the cathedral districts of some cities preserves the memory of this skill and the men who performed it.

✦ The mortar mixer was seldom left out of pictorial evocations of the medieval building-sites.

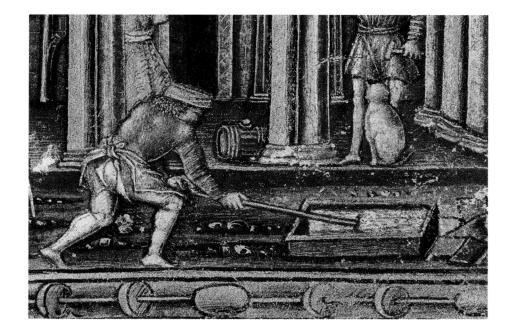

+ *Left:* The mortar was very often mixed near the building site.

## On the Difference between Masonry and Stonecutting

At the cathedral building-sites, which varied greatly, distinctions and specializations were not always clearly established. Until the fifteenth century, it was fairly common to find workers who in winter labored in the quarry as stonecutters and when summer came worked as masons on the building site. Confusion of vocabulary also reached its height when some masters of the works or architects began to be referred to as either *capitalis cementarius* or *capitalis lathomus*.

And yet, the distinction between stonecutters and masons remains a significant element in the analysis of the stone crafts that participated in the construction of the cathedral. If the art of the mortar mixer was now clearly identified and identifiable, the terms used to describe the other crafts related to stone must be analyzed frequently in order that the subtlety of the specialization of techniques and skills may be grasped. Thus, in England, the hewer was distinguished from the layer; in Germany, the *Maurer* (mason) was distinguished from the *Steinmetz* (cutter). Words such as *cubitores* and *positores* (layers, posers) had their equivalent in France in the term *asseyeurs,* crafts-

men who were charged with placing the stones down, laying them flat, and cementing them to the others.

In the middle of the fourteenth century, a new vocabulary was invented in England, which was destined for subsequent reinterpretations and new uses: "free" masons were distinguished from rough or ordinary masons. Everywhere in Europe that cathedrals were being built, a clear differentiation took place between two categories of workers who, in the hierarchical ladder of the different trades, appeared on a much higher rung than the one on which the mortar mixer generally stood. There was the "superior" mason, who knew how to cut the stones, and the "less important mason," whose abilities were restricted to merely laying stones at the building site. The word *cementarius* persisted for quite some time to describe these two crafts before giving way, once and for all, to the term "mason."

This distinction quite logically led to disputes over precedence among communities of builders. Was it the craft of the stonecutter or the stone layer that was more noble, that is, more important, because it was the more difficult? The length of the apprenticeship

+ *Below:* The trowel, the mason's emblematic tool.

◆ Man at prayer, man at war, man at work: the cathedral was at the center of medieval life.

was often a very relevant indicator. Reading the medieval statutes and other regulations, we detect the implied supremacy of the stonecutters over the masons (an apprenticeship of five years in the former case, three years in the latter). Another aspect to be analyzed, the salaries, seems to confirm the predominance of those who had the skill to cut

stones over those who only knew how to lay them. On some building sites, the wages paid varied from the same to double the amount, but it is difficult and unwise to generalize from the few cases that are known. Thus, the accounts of the Autun workshop committee give a daily salary of ten deniers to the mortar mixers, while the masons and stonecutters seem to be grouped together and earned around twenty deniers each. Régine Pernoud considers that masons or stonecutters in the thirteenth century spent a third of their pay on food and that the wages they received allowed them to live very comfortably if they were single, quite well if they were married and had one child.

There are other echoes of this rivalry between the two aristocracies of craftsmen in stone, such as the struggle between the masons and stonecutters of Strasbourg who, at the beginning of the fifteenth century, disagreed over who was to keep the banner of the emblems of the corporation, the *Zunft*—a symbolic dispute over stakes or trophies that is of more than anecdotal interest to us. The Statutes of Ratisbon, which were adopted in 1459, were also supposed to regulate matters of precedence between stonecutters and masons throughout the whole of Europe.

Gradually, the "high crafts" became more and more concerned with officially declaring, if not their exclusive supremacy, then at least their importance and prestige. Stone, wood, and to a

## On the Subject of Salaries

Although it is not possible to establish any general rule that was respected on all the cathedral building-sites, we can discern a number of general principles that characterized them. Two forms of remuneration were practiced: a fixed sum for piecework, and a daily wage. But things were not as simple as that, as is shown by the many extras often described in the account books. Supplementary rations of wine, food, or firewood were given out when a worker had to remain on the site for a prolonged period of time. Additional payments were granted to the master of the works to cover the cost of his bed and lodgings for the year. The many variations in the salary scales make for difficult and complex reading of a time before any collective agreements had been implemented.

Be that as it may, it is true to say that in every country the stonecutters, masons, carpenters, blacksmiths, and glass artists were the most important and highest-paid groups.

lesser degree metal defined the fundamental trio of the major crafts practiced in building a cathedral. This phenomenon of precedence or hierarchy was to reappear in the history of French craft-guilds until the end of the nineteenth century, when stonecutters and carpenters fought, sometimes quite violently, over the title of "Lords of the Craftsmen." Manuscript miniatures and other medieval paintings give the best positions to the workers in wood or stone, their crafts being the most visible, and therefore also the most prominent in pictorial art. This should not be allowed to obscure the crafts that were less visible but just as important to the work on the cathedral.

If the mason's primary function was to raise the walls by placing stone upon stone, the stonecutter's mission was a more delicate one. From the eleventh century on, he was the principal player in an extremely important technical revolution. It was because of him that a rough architecture based on stones broken with a hammer gave way to dressed-stone construction, in which the joints and grooves between the blocks were made smaller. The knowledge of geometry formed the true division between the majority of masons, or bricklayers, and the stonecutters. A large number of technicians and architects were very knowledgeable about stone and how it was cut, and having this knowledge was essential to anyone who aspired to become a master of the works or an architect. The workshops of the stonecutters, true schools of great architects, formed communities that were distinct from those of the so-called ordinary masons. This was the case in both Germany and France.

✦ The legend of Saint Bertin, painted in Dijon by Lancelot Blondeel, also evokes the daily life of the stone- and woodworkers.

◆ Sultan Omar rebuilds the Temple (Guillaume de Tyr. From *Histoire de la conquête de Jérusalem.* Fifteenth century). Another example of the symbolic transferral of the Gothic cathedral to the Temple of Jerusalem— a model of perfection created by the medieval imagination.

## Foreigners and Itinerants

Thus the geographic origins of the cathedral builders were, at least partly, described. While the laborers and mortar mixers were generally recruited locally, the cathedral cities were not able to supply sufficient numbers of masons and stonecutters to the building sites. Based on the studies of the French, British, and German scholars who have seriously examined this subject, we can say that only 5 to 10 percent of the workers were from the region where the construction site was located. The terms "foreigners" (*étrangers*) and "itinerants" (*passants*), which appear so often in the legends and other records of the French craftsmen's guilds, were used with their original meaning, to describe a specialized workforce that did a

lot of traveling. Every stonecutter who arrived in a city and came to work at the cathedral building-site was a foreigner. The local population knew that he would only stay temporarily, that once his work had been completed he would move to another building site. That is why he was also called an itinerant or passerby. But this phenomenon was not new and was by no means restricted to the building sites of the Gothic cathedrals. From the sixth century on, masons, stonecutters, as well as carpenters and glassworkers crossed frontiers in response to invitations from patrons who would pay them for working on a building site that was in some way special. This simple fact raises the question of the reputation of an architect and his school, the existence and the quality of which

## The Diversity of the Stonecutters

There was no single, universal profile of the stonecutter. As in the cases of the cathedrals, building sites, and lodges, we must diversify an image that has for too long been reduced to an excessively simple model. The stonecutters were a group of workers who varied in terms of their qualifications and in terms of the stone they worked on, the tools that were available to them, and the training they received.

While we have little information that might help us understand the diversity and nature of their initial training, the inventories of some lodges do point out the existence of two categories: either the tools were provided by the workshop, as in Milan, or the workers had to provide their own equipment.

In 1399, the inventory of the lodge in York mentions the presence there of sixty-nine large hammers, ninety-six iron chisels, twenty-four medium hammers, two drawing boards, two buckets, two carts, one small ax, one handsaw, one pair of dividers, one shovel, one crowbar, and one wheelbarrow. D. Knoop and G. P. Jones, who have analyzed this inventory, rightly note the absence of set squares, levels, and plumb lines, and they conclude that those tools must have belonged to the people who used them in their work.

Graduated rulers, hammers, chisels, levers, skeleton keys, dividers, set squares—each lodge required appropriate tools, which were often passed from father to son or more frequently were manufactured with the help of the blacksmith or the carpenter.

*Left:* Many of the stained-glass windows of cathedrals (here, Bourges) glorify the corporations, especially those relating to the stoneworkers.

were known thousands of miles from the place where they were based. In fact, all builders' schools were, by definition, mobile. A genuine construction company, such a school did have a head office, where it was possible to apply to be admitted to the school. Religion was also linked to the world of the construction workers, as bishops and abbots sometimes acted as intermediaries between employers and employees.

The stonecutters in particular were defined by this culture of travel. From the thirteenth century onward, the Cistercian abbeys could be described as genuine recruitment, placement, and hiring agencies, so skilled the disciples of Bernard de Clairvaux were at making use of these "mercenaries," who turned out to be not all of the stoneworkers, but at least the best of them.

Being mobile, free, and independent, part of the workforce of the cathedral projects did not subscribe to the same rules as those that were in effect in the corporations, which were by definition sedentary institutions, and they therefore formed communities of builders who were totally free of the corporate shackles of the cities. The cathedral building-sites should also be analyzed primarily in terms of the distinction that was made between the traveling and the stable workers, as this was an essential feature of the craftsmen's world in the Middle Ages.

♦ Among all the ironworking crafts, edge-tool making has always occupied a preeminent position in the manufacture of cutting tools. This tool is known as a boucharde.

# Sculptors and Modelmakers

## The Stonecutter's Training

Even today, it is not at all easy to establish a very clear distinction between the sculptors and the stonecutters who worked on the cathedral projects. Except in Italy, the word "sculptor" is quite seldom found. Like Pierre du Colombier, the present writer believes that the sculptors of the cathedrals were none other than stonecutters whose special skills and talents for dressing and decorating stone and making the stones into sculptures were recognized. In certain miniatures (the most famous being Fouquet's), the "sculptor" is shown surrounded by a group of stonecutters, with one very clear distinguishing sign: he is the only one wearing a white band around his head.

To discover the nature or function of a specific craft, we need only consult the account books or ledgers of the cathedrals, which are quite enlightening on the subject. In fact, as a general rule, these ledgers tend to confirm that few distinctions were made between the trades of stonecutter and sculptor. On the building site in Milan in 1481, for example, the companions were paid ten sous when they worked on the ground and twelve if they had to work on scaffolding sculpting decorations. It is clear that everywhere in Europe, the sculptor was an ordinary stonecutter who nonetheless had to be paid a higher salary because of his talents in the art of sculpture. In the German lodges, the stonecutters were usually trained as sculptors.

✦ Plaster, stone, wood—statuary was made in several different materials. Here, *Saint Angadreme*, in the cathedral of Saint-Pierre in Beauvais.

## The Sculptor at Work

We have seen that many blocks were rough-hewn on the site of the quarry to reduce by as much as possible the costs involved in transporting the stone. Delicate sculptures were, however, only very rarely executed at the quarry because of the obvious risks of damaging the work during transit. Nevertheless, there were sculptors' workshops very close to some quarries that specialized in the production of small pieces, whole sets of which were made there; columns, capitals, or low reliefs could also, at least in part, be sculpted at the quarry. Knoop and Jones mention, for example, a workshop in England where large quantities of heads of Saint John the Baptist were made. They have also found evidence of the presence of small lodges that were situated within the quarries themselves, but these cases were extremely rare and marginal.

As a general rule, the sculptor received a block that had already been chiseled down, and he modeled and carved it into shape on the cathedral building-site, within the lodge, or out in the open, if this work did not reveal too many of the secrets and techniques of his art. Medieval miniatures show the sculptor working in two distinct settings: in the lodge and in the open air. In many cases, the block to be worked on is shown lying on its side or leaning gently against another object. Up until the sixteenth century, it seems to have been standard practice to carve statues in this way; the sculpture never appears standing up in the paintings.

To this day, scholars are divided over the question of whether the sculptor worked from patterns, drawings, or even models. We do know, however, that a number of full-size plaster models were made for the sculptor to follow, and in such instances he was a true copyist. The same applies to the drawings, which guided or even dictated the work that was to be carried out; many of these are still in existence. Similarly heated debates center around the degree to which the sculptor had any freedom in relation to both the commission he was given and the patterns he could choose.

From the time of the Second Nicean Council and the famous "Quarrel of the Images" (at the end of the eighth and beginning of the ninth centuries, respectively), the faithful were reminded that the only images that could be exhibited in churches were those that were accepted by tradition and had been approved by the priest in charge of each church, in other words, by the patron commissioning the work. But throughout the Middle Ages, sculptors and other artists had always been able to preserve a degree of creative independence when faced with the requirements of an authority that could impose a subject but could not dictate how it was to be realized.

◆ *Below:* As illustrated by the famous gargoyles at the cathedral of Notre-Dame in Paris, freedom and creativity characterized the work of the specialized sculptor, a master of his art.

◆ *Pages 108–9:* A detail of the rood screen in the cathedral of Sainte-Cécile, Albi. Few French cathedrals have preserved such a complete rood screen.

There are many churches, basilicas, and cathedrals all over Europe that testify to the freedom and even the daring of some sculptors who found ways of getting around rigid ecclesiastical or artistic guidelines; the gargoyles on the cathedrals clearly remind us of that fact.

The sculptor would take measurements with the help of dividers, trace lines and cut the blocks of stone with the tip of his hammer, and further detail the stone with chisels, which he would strike with a mallet. In winter, laboring in the heated lodge, the sculptor did not have to interrupt his work, as the mason did. He was one of the people who formed the stable nucleus of the cathedral-building team, assuming the workshop's finances were healthy and the workshop committee could afford to pay many workers throughout the year.

## Sculpture in Full Color

Once it was completed, medieval sculpture was embellished with colors that were meant to make the work more beautiful and to appear more striking to the faithful. The sculptors only seldom painted their sculptures; it was the painters who took care of this very precise and delicate task.

Already in use for wooden sculptures, painting gave an added dimension to a piece; it did not assume its definitive symbolic and practical functions until it was polychromatic. Thus, today, we look at sculptures that the Christians of medieval times were bound to see differently, simply because they saw them in color.

The painters' palette was quite extensive and included red, pink, blue, black, green, white, and gold. These colors were only rarely applied directly onto the stone; a type of ceruse preparation was applied to the work before it was painted.

◆ A scene on the construction site of an imaginary cathedral of Notre-Dame, as envisioned by illustrator Philippe Fix.

# Carpenters and the Wood Crafts

## The Supremacy of Stone

In the opinion of many medievalists, the scarcity and the rise in the price of suitable wood in the twelfth and thirteenth centuries (which were the consequences of overexploitation or misuse of the forests in the tenth and eleventh centuries) explain, to a very large extent, the definitive victory of stone in building projects. This assertion must, however, be modified, depending on which countries and regions we are studying. England, for example, having much greater and much higher quality areas of forest than France, has a number of buildings in which the carpenters were able to show the full range of their skills. The wooden spire of Salisbury Cathedral and the lantern tower of Ely Cathedral reveal the amazing talent of the English carpenters. But the victory of stone over wood also came about because stone was fireproof, impervious to termites, and much more resistant to impact and bad weather. In spite of the financial problems that were associated, above all, with transporting it, stone would now appear much more competitive than wood, on the large-scale construction sites that grew up around the Gothic cathedrals as they were being built.

In spite of the triumph of stone, wood remained an indispensable material for the construction of the framework of the roof, arches, scaffolding, platforms, and lifting machines and equipment, without which the stones could not reach the tops of the buildings that were growing taller and taller. Two instruments that had been used since ancient times would now undergo significant modifications.

The famous hoist described by Vitruvius was gradually transformed into a crane by the use of a counterweight and a double pulley. Carpenters placed it on the ground or on a platform, depending on the height of the building. Some cranes pivoted, allowing a savings of time and increased efficiency. When the weight was not too great, a simple hook was sufficient to get hold of the stone and raise it.

The treadmill, which was operated by two laborers who made it rotate by walking inside

♦ A treadmill and claw, as depicted by an anonymous draftsman in a fifteenth-century engineer's manual.

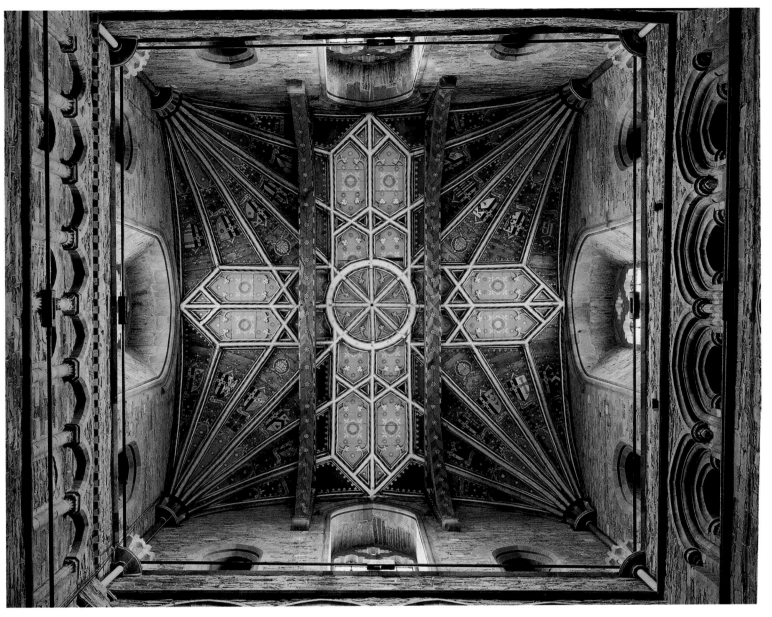

◆ Saint David's Cathedral, the tower seen from below, where the wood is hidden from the gaze of the visitor.

the wheel, allowed very sizable weights to be lifted because of a claw that held up the stone that was being raised. Alain Erlande-Brandenburg tells us that a single man standing in a treadmill two and a half yards in diameter could lift up to thirteen hundred pounds. Treadmills were easy to make and could conveniently be dismantled, set up again, and moved from one part of the building site to another. Sometimes a treadmill ended up in the attic of the cathedral, as in Salisbury, where it is still possible to see it. In Beauvais, Châlons-en-Charny, and several other religious sites, the treadmill is also still visible, above the transept vaults.

On the cathedral building-site, carpenters were primarily makers of lifting equipment. These lifting machines were the instruments of a considerable revolution, which made a significant contribution to the definition of Gothic architecture. They marked the end of the need for the heavy scaffolding that was so prominent in the Romanesque period. From now on, as the raising of the building progressed, workers moved about by means of spiral staircases, which the architect had planned from the beginning of the project. The construction of rib vaults did not require scaffolding to be placed on the ground, since they were built between one wall and another, which provided the very wide working surfaces that were necessary to temporarily support the heavy wooden arches. These could be dismantled and used over and over again as the work continued.

✦ The wooden roof-structure of the cathedral of Notre-Dame, Paris.

# *The Carpenters*

*A journeyman carpenter, Raoul Vergez, known as "the Béarnais who was the Friend of the Tour of France," describes the wooden framework of the roof of Notre-Dame Cathedral, in Paris:*

Of the immense network of oaks and chestnuts that now make up the roof timbers of the cathedral, with their rooftop gangways and labyrinths that are so vast that they are referred to as "the forest," only the section that overlooks the chevet over the headland of the Cité belongs to the ancient woodwork. The trees that make up its circular array must have grown in the forests of the Ile-de-France, at the time of Saint Bernard, when work on the cathedral had not even begun. Those people who have doubts about the longevity of these venerable wooden columns should visit these amazing assemblies of enormous beams that float like ships above the medieval arches. . . .

The iconography of the masons' guilds of earliest times was incised with a small tool that made the grooves in the core of oaks appear on the tree trunks that were sawn with a handsaw and felled with a felling ax, in the curves of the arched surface of beams that had been laid flat or vertically, and in the engraved patterns and ragged edges of the planks. The skilled woodcutters who had come from Normandy, Burgundy, or Gascony literally illuminated the forest of Notre-Dame with those same magical signs that their ancestors had used on the upturned ship of Bourges or of Cluny.

—Raoul Vergez, *Bois d'aujourd'hui*

## Architecture Came from the Sea

In his *Dictionnaire raisonné de l'architecture française du XIème au XVIème siècle* (Encyclopedic dictionary of French architecture from the eleventh to the sixteenth century), Eugène-Emmanuel Viollet-le-Duc draws a parallel between naval carpentry and that of the Gothic cathedrals: "In England, for example, it is well known that all the great wooden buildings of the fourteenth and fifteenth centuries, many of which are still standing, have much in common with the art of naval carpentry. The wooden roof frameworks, their relative forces, and the frequent use of curves constantly recall, in our mind, the techniques of carpentry that were used in ships." The great architect was simply stating an observation that has since been proven historically: in countries like Great Britain and regions such as Normandy, areas where seafaring traditions were strong, carpenters doubled as builders of ships and of the naves of churches. A comparison between the cathedral and an upturned ship, and consideration of the French word *nef,* which means vessel or ship but is also used to describe the nave of a church, reveal some of the strong links that once existed between naval and cathedral carpenters.

◆ *Above:* Naval carpenters in India.

◆ *Right:* The roof framework of the cathedral of Bourges.

◆ This carpenter's adze could be disassembled for easy transport.

◆ *Pages 116–17:* Ely Cathedral, the octagon. In 1322, following the collapse of part of the lantern tower of the cathedral, the carpenter William Hurley attempted to imitate stone by the illusionistic use of wood. He employed a two-level system of pointed arches. The light weight of wood enabled the carpenters to open up a large space, with two rows of windows allowing it to be admirably well lit.

◆ *Page 119:* The operation of small-scale cranes was a task generally entrusted to the apprentice (recognizable by his stockings, which stop at the knees), under the supervision of a companion.

## Seasoned Wood and Green Wood

As soon as the masons had erected the walls of the nave or transept, the carpenters constructed the wooden framework of the roof, which the roofers quickly covered over to protect the interior from rain. The masons could then build the vaults sheltered from bad weather. The carpenters were also involved in this job. Wooden arches were indispensable in supporting the stones of the vaults or arches while they were being assembled and while the mortar dried. In the Gothic period, instead of being destroyed after each use, the wood arches were carefully dismantled and then put together again for the construction of the next arch. Thus wood was saved and all the arches would look the same.

Unlike cabinetmakers, who needed very dry and seasoned wood from which to build their furniture, carpenters almost exclusively used unseasoned or green wood. A study of the account books indicates that cabinetmakers or joiners could buy dry wood from specialized merchants and foreign traders; Spanish supplies were among the best. This need to work with dry wood is easily explained: the wood had to be reliable, it could not be subject to rapid warping or other unwanted changes. The recorded dates when timber was cut, transported, and worked on confirm that the carpenters did, by contrast, frequently seek out green wood. The practice was not employed on all the building sites, but a number of medievalists, including Odette Chapelot, have emphasized how widespread it really was.

The great cathedral construction-sites were huge consumers of wood, and they required larger quantities of timber than were locally available. Having a supply of dry wood at hand presupposed the existence of a permanent stock that had been kept in storage for decades. Most cities did not have such a stock because they had neither the time nor the money to store it.

Unseasoned wood did not cause major problems in the manufacture of arches, coffering, scaffolding, or lifting equipment. But the situation was very different in the case of the wooden framework of the roof, where premature warping would require that those pieces be constantly maintained. Such warping was caused not by a lack of expertise on the part of the carpenters but by the methods employed in producing and preparing the timber, which were still very much those of a cottage industry.

◆ *Right:* The bevel was used to measure corners and other angles.

## From Noah's Ark to the Tower of Babel

After reigning as masters until the eleventh century, in the thirteenth century carpenters were finally obliged to acknowledge the supremacy of masons and stonecutters. The fine wooden roof frameworks that they built, which were the product of great technical skill, remain hidden from the gaze of pilgrims and other visitors by the stone vaults that drew heavily on the woodworking crafts while relegating them to a secondary position. The carpenters' pride therefore sought refuge in the spires of the cathedrals, those genuine masterpieces that presupposed an extremely sophisticated art of tracery and fine woodwork. While fires have destroyed the most ornate spires in France (Reims, Chartres, and Rouen), some very remarkable examples have fortunately been preserved in England, such as the one that still adorns Salisbury Cathedral.

When the craftsmen of the Gothic age discovered the possibility of creating vaults without using wooden arches, especially in the lower parts of the roof, the woodworking arts experienced the final assault of an age that marked a major shift in the heritage and culture of

the manual trades. In the duke of Bedford's book of hours, a miniature depicting the building of Noah's Ark is nothing less than the building site of a wooden house that is being erected by men belonging to the brotherhood of woodworkers. They labor under the orders of Noah, who is depicted as the master of the works. Contrasted with this great building site celebrating wood alone is another whose character is just as mythical: that of the Tower of Babel, which glorifies exclusively a different material, stone. Traditional lore, too, perpetuates this duality of stone and wood, which has marked our collective memory to such an extent that it slips into our most famous fairy-tales, such as the story of Tom Thumb, in which the children get lost in the forest and find their way again with the help of a trail of small pebbles.

It is worth stressing again that the Gothic cathedrals could not have been built without the collaboration of master carpenters and masons, who were all involved in determining the height and width of the building. A book of stone and of glass, the cathedral was never universally recognized also as a book of wood.

# Plasterers, Roofers, and Plumbers

In the regions rich in gypsum, such as the Ile-de-France (the region around Paris), the cathedrals benefited from the expertise of the plasterers. It is quite clear that the plasterers of the Gothic period were well aware of the potential of plaster, in spite of its poor resistance to water. Plaster could be molded in any number of ways and was therefore utilized in the coffering of ceilings. It also proved to be very useful in stonework, particularly for joints and pointing, thus forming the perfect interior covering for the vaults.

For the roof of the cathedral, roofers were no longer using wood, which had been abandoned because of the danger of fire. The example of lightning is always cited, but people too often forget the risks associated with the presence of candles in churches. Nonetheless, the roofers stayed in close contact with the carpenters because they had to adapt their work to the developments taking place in the wooden frameworks of the roofs. In France, they would have to wait until 1321 to benefit from the true independence that was marked by the granting of their own statutes, which freed them from the supervision of the carpenters.

However, many problems were posed by the use of stone. It took a very long time to complete a stone roof. Moreover, the walls of the cathedral, which might have collapsed under the weight of the roof, had to be supported. Buttresses thus had to be designed and paid for. In order to make the roof watertight, lead, slate, or flat stone tiles were often used, according to the region where the building site was located. Depending on their surface texture and the direction in which they were laid, slate allowed the roofers to create different effects, forming two-toned mosaics that could be admired from a distance. Lead could be decorated by applying paint directly to it.

The corporation of plumbers was directly dependent on that of the roofers. Although they executed masterful works—ornamental crests, ornate pinnacles, and hammered or chiseled work in repoussé—whose excellence is also recognized today, they did not have the privilege of being one of the "high crafts" associated with the cathedral because their work was, unfortunately, the least visible and the least accessible to visitors.

◆ *Above:* Saint Guthlac constructing a chapel, as shown in a twelfth-century drawing on parchment.

◆ *Right:* The cathedral of Amiens. The top surfaces of the flying buttresses are channeled so that rainwater will drain off and away from the building.

Starting with an ingot of lead, plumbers prepared, in the workshop or in the open air, sheets with which to finish the roof. This block of lead was heated until it was molten and was then poured into a flat mold, the bottom of which was dusted with sand. The lead cooled into heavy yet flexible sheets generally not more than one yard wide and several yards long. The master plumber and his team could then assemble and fix them onto the roof of the cathedral. Rolled around wooden posts, these sheets could also become pipes and gutters. But the price of lead was such that roofers sometimes preferred to use tile or slate instead. These materials were much lighter than the tiles that the Romans used or than the stones that came from mountainous regions, and they were just as resistant to fire, the cathedral's persistent earthly enemy.

The roofer also had to devise an appropriate arrangement of channels and gargoyles to carry rainwater off and away from the building. Gutters were generally hidden within the buttresses and pinnacles. As for the stone gargoyles, they were the object of artistic creation that often went beyond the bishop's or the chief architect's initial designs. Sculpted in the form of monsters or demons, they sometimes showed in daring detail a more human face, which was supposed to portray a powerful person or the artist himself.

✦ Gargoyles, products of human imagination and creativity, as well as functional elements: placed at the ends of flying buttresses at Chartres, they served as spouts through which rainwater flowed.

# Blacksmiths and Locksmiths

On the cathedral construction-sites, the metal crafts were generally practiced by both blacksmiths and locksmiths. It seems, however, that on many sites no clear distinction was made between these two professions, which were usually not itinerant crafts, unlike that of the stone-cutters. We should nonetheless be careful not to confuse two crafts that were profoundly different in spite of their common dependence on a forge, which was fired by charcoal and appeared on all the building sites.

Although they were also one of the frequently overlooked links in the chain of craftsmen, blacksmiths were constantly present on the cathedral building-sites. It was to them that one turned when tools had to be repaired or sharpened. The use of iron was widespread. It was used, for example, for the joints between blocks of marble, as was the case, for example, in Milan Cathedral. Lead sometimes served a similar purpose. The most costly hard metal seems to have been steel, which was used for the manufacture of pickaxes and cold chisels and therefore needed to be very resilient and tempered.

Progress and new developments in the blacksmith's craft contributed to making the tasks of the main participants in the Gothic building projects easier. By fashioning tools out of more and more resistant types of steel, the blacksmiths enabled harder and harder types of stone to be cut, stones that until then could not have been used by builders. The stonecutter's hammer, which probably first appeared in the course of the twelfth century, was recognized as a major innovation. Thanks to the blacksmiths, too, carpenters benefited from more effective tools, such as saws and adzes, which favored the creation of increasingly elaborate wooden frameworks, arches, and scaffolding made from harder woods. Now that more resistant types of stone and more durable

✦ *Left:* A forge, as shown in a detail of a sixteenth-century painting illustrating the Tower of Babel.

✦ *Opposite:* The ambulatory of the cathedral of Saint-Julien in Le Mans. The portal, made of forged iron, was reconstructed in the eighteenth century.

✦ *Right:* Vulcan, the master of the forge with mysterious powers, as depicted in a fifteenth-century miniature.

kinds of wood could be used, architects could design columns that were narrower in diameter and walls that were thinner. Sculptors and carvers were also grateful to the blacksmiths for tools that at last enabled them to realize finer and more delicate designs.

On the cathedral building-site, the blacksmith was also required to supply not only all kinds of nails but also the vital horseshoes and metal harness parts for the draft animals. As in the Sainte-Chapelle, in Paris, the architect also turned to the blacksmith for the famous iron chains that were to be sealed within the stonework to reinforce the walls. Unfortunately, in many cases, these chains would turn out to be truly terrible enemies, causing numerous cracks to appear in the building. For Soissons Cathedral, from the end of the twelfth century, iron was used to make tie-rods, which were installed in the southern part

◆ *Above:* Metal was indispensable to the construction and maintenance of the great rose windows. Here, the cathedral of Notre-Dame, Paris.

◆ *Opposite:* Well before the Gothic era, ironworkers were already making fine doors such as this Romanesque example.

of the transept and in the nave to compensate for the thrust of the vaults. Tensioning connectors situated at the center of each tie-rod allowed each iron bar to be tightened or loosened. This system of tie-rods is also found in the Sainte-Chapelle.

From the thirteenth century on, metal also enabled the construction of rose windows of enormous diameters—forty-two feet in the case of Notre-Dame Cathedral in Paris. Wood and stone thus gave way to metal in certain very specific situations. In Carcassonne and Strasbourg, some of the windows are held in place by a metal framework that the architect endeavored to hide from view. Metal was used more and more often to solve problems of stability. From Vézelay to Soissons,

Beauvais to Dijon, it contributed significantly to the triumph of the Gothic style by providing reinforcement and stability, without which the movement could not have flourished so fully.

The ornamental ironwork of the cathedral doors was entrusted to specialists. In France, the corporation of iron blacksmiths was regularly asked to manufacture and maintain the heavy doors of the cathedral. Makers of patterns in iron, the locksmiths were also responsible for the locks and keys that protected the treasures and relics kept in many of the cathedrals. In the Kingdom of France, the corporation's statutes specified, from the thirteenth century, that "no key was to be made without having the lock before one's eyes."

# Glass Artists and Glassworkers

### The Cathedral: From the Book of Stone to the Book of Glass

One way of looking at Gothic architecture is to say that it was characterized by a reduction in the surface area of the masonry walls constituting the building. Bays and windows became larger, and stained glass was used plentifully in the spaces

✦ These stained-glass windows in Bourges reveal the full extent of the talent of the glassmaker, which assumes many years of training, great sensitivity, and a mastery of the art.

once occupied by walls. The cathedral was gradually transformed from a book of stone into a book
of glass. This was the case in the nave of the Sainte-
Chapelle, where only the minimal amount of masonry was used; the rest of the wall surfaces are
alive with luminous images. This revolution favored the elaboration of vast programs illustrating

Christian thought of the period as well as the devotions that were specific to a particular church or community.

As it made use of light, the stained-glass window was welcomed by theologians, who wanted to see in the church, which was both a functional and a symbolic entity, the image and embodiment of the heavenly Jerusalem, sparkling with a thousand colors. Thus Guillaume de Mende, in his *Manuel des divins offices* (Manual of divine services) did not hesitate to compare the stained-glass windows to divine Scriptures, "which pour the clarity of the true sun, that is, of God in the Church, into the hearts of the faithful, thereby enlightening them."

◆ Glassblowers portrayed in an Italian miniature from the fifteenth century.

The stained-glass window gradually replaced the fresco, while serving the same purpose as it and as sculpture: to transmit a message, a lesson, to those who could not read. A book of stone, a book of images, a book of glass, the cathedral revealed itself to many different kinds of readers, cultured or ignorant, powerful or humble, all of whom were attracted by an extraordinary building that called out to each of its visitors by means of a large number of pictorial representations that stimulated meditation and reflection on mysteries, to which the Church was believed to hold the keys.

## Stained-glass Windows, Rose Windows, and Walls of Glass

The master glass-artist was, first and foremost, the executor of a work that had been commissioned and conceived by the chapter and bishop for theological and pedagogical purposes.

A unique case is that of Chartres Cathedral, which houses the most remarkable stained-glass windows of the Gothic period. The cathedral has 160 windows and three rose windows, the first of which were made around 1200, and the most recent ones around 1235 to 1240. Celebrating the glory of the Virgin Mary, Saint Anne, and Christ, these stained-glass windows and rose windows vie with each other in beauty and splendor, to establish and proclaim the link between the Bible and the Christian people. But stained-glass windows were not commissioned only for and by the church. Powerful individuals and corporations considered it their duty to have their own stained-glass windows in the sacred building as well. Such a window was a symbol of protection, of belonging to the great Christian family, but it was also a concrete expression of the real concern to celebrate one's financial success or declare one's social status. It reveals the glory of a craft and is a work of art that must be admired in its own right. In a very few cases, the corporation's stained-glass window has its origin in some other purpose; for example, the winegrowers of Le Mans had to donate a stained-glass window to the cathedral because they arrived late at the ceremony at which the cathedral's new choir was consecrated, on

April 20, 1254. Whether they were donated or required, all these windows became privileged expressions of the corporations' history. Unlike the nobles and clergy, who usually chose a prayerful attitude, the members of the crafts and trades were always portrayed in the midst of activity, on the building site or in the workshop. In this respect, Chartres is a true repository of the techniques and tools of the medieval crafts, as these are all represented in the beautiful, rich stained-glass windows that were paid for by the corporations

Since the price of a stained-glass window was high, church dignitaries, monks, noblemen, and lords most commonly financed the work of the glass artists. In return, they were often portrayed in the window, and they were careful not to forget to have their names and titles mentioned by having them engraved in the form of signatures. A generous donor was also sometimes depicted in the window. If such representations had not been included, the names of these important individuals of the period would have completely disappeared from the people's collective memory.

## The Traveling Schools and Workshops

In the thirteenth-century cathedral, the number of windows to be glazed was generally so large that it was fairly common for those in

✦ The stained-glass windows in Chartres Cathedral do not merely proclaim the glory of the builders' crafts. Many of them, such as these two depicting fur and cloth merchants, were financed by corporations to secure divine protection and to display to the Christian people their economic success, the proceeds of which they then reinvested in the cathedral building. It was customary to commission either a whole window or part of one.

◆ *Opposite:* The upper chapel of the Sainte-Chapelle in Paris is one of the best places in which to appreciate the excellence of the work of the stained-glass artists and the perfect harmony achieved between glass and stone.

◆ *Below:* Detail of a stained-glass window in Canterbury Cathedral depicting the death of Saint Martin.

charge of the workshop to have to ask several master glass-artists to collaborate on the cathedral construction-site. The number of stained-glass windows produced in the thirteenth century was so great that we find many different techniques used in the windows of a single building.

Looking for new projects to work on, glass artists would come to the site from far away and leave as soon as their work had been completed. Some workshops, such as those of the Laon or Soissons regions, did not hesitate to travel from one building site to another, spreading skills that were much in demand. The master of the works or architect looked out for respected artists whom he was willing to pay handsomely. Thus, in the case of the abbey church of Saint-Denis, Abbot Suger notes that "he had very carefully searched for makers of stained-glass windows and of glass, who used such exquisite materials, such as large numbers of sapphires which they crushed and melted in with the glass, to give it the azure-blue color that really aroused his delight and admiration. For this reason, he had the most subtle and skilled masters brought from foreign countries in order to create painted windows for the chapel of the Virgin and for the bays above the main door of the church." Suger even specifies that "he had appointed as the head of this project an expert master of this art and a number of clerics who were to oversee the work and look after the workers, supplying them with all that they needed as and when they needed it. These windows cost him a lot because of the excellence and the scarcity of the materials of which they were made."

The work of the glass artists Suger recruited seems to have elicited the admiration of the Christian people because they also helped finance the windows: "When it enabled these windows to be made, the devotion of the people, both great and small, was so intense that so much money appeared in the collection boxes that there was enough of it to pay the workers at the end of each week."

In the thirteenth century, the composition and the style of a stained-glass window varied according to the region, the workshop, and even the artist, whose designs grew directly out of his

# Stained-Glass Windows

The people of the Gothic age did not invent this form of art; glasswork had been introduced by the Romans. But in their civic and religious architecture, those craftsmen of the Gothic age were the precursors of the people who create the glass walls of today.

For centuries, glass had been a luxury material in buildings, and very few examples of it were found. According to one legend, Saint Wilfred used glass in the restoration of the church in York, in the second half of the seventh century. At that time, it was to Gaul that people went when they were looking for glass. In England, the oilcloth was still in standard use for window coverings as late as the thirteenth century, but glass was beginning to be used more widely. In 1243, King Henry III of England had the oilcloths in his chancellery replaced by glass. In 1238, glass was ordered to be placed over the wire mesh of the windows "to prevent drafts."

The use of this new element of comfort had become so widespread that in the thirteenth century the Cistercians reacted against such luxury by forbidding the use of glass in their churches.

But from the tenth century onward, the art of the stained-glass window had also been developed, especially in France, as is revealed by a treatise written by the monk Théophile, *De diversis artibus,* which was the first technical manual of the Middle Ages. Cut up by means of a red-hot iron point, pieces of different-colored glass were fitted into a lead framework, forming a luminous mosaic. The later development of painting on glass would completely alter the original vigorous style, by blending several colors on a single fragment of glass.

—Roland Bechmann,
*Les Racines des cathédrales*

◆ At Chartres, the stained glass also evokes the daily life and labors of the peasants. Here, threshing wheat in August.

particular training and influence. The art of the stained-glass window was thus constantly evolving.

The glass artist was a craftsman who generally remained anonymous; thus few names have come down to us. Apart from Clément, from Chartres; Etienne, from Bourges; and a few other master glass-artists whose signatures we can see in the stained-glass windows or in the account ledgers of the thirteenth century, few traces of these masters of light remain.

## The Work of the Glass Artist

We know that the glass artists also had a workshop that was situated just a few yards away from the cathedral building-site. As with the stone- and woodcrafts, the glass workers were organized in a lodge that was directed by a workshop manager or master.

Glassworking was very slow and deliberate. Contrary to a commonly held belief, master glass-artists did not make the glass itself, which was supplied directly to them by the glassmakers. These workers often had their workshops in the country, on the edges of forests. Glass was obtained by heating, in a wood fire at almost 1,500°C, a blend of one part river sand to two parts fern and beechwood ashes.

Once he had a supply of raw materials, the glass artist carried out his work entirely in the shelter of his workshop. Here, as elsewhere, the secrets of the craft were jealously guarded. The master, helped by his companions, began by drawing the "cartoon," a full-size pattern of the stained-glass window to be executed. Then came the cutting of the glass. The master artist (or the companion glass-cutter) placed the glass carefully onto a table that had been sprinkled with chalk dust, and then cut it using the point of a knife that had been heated in the fire. Glass was not cut with diamonds until the sixteenth century. It was a work of transparency, whose every detail was drawn and then, by means of the cutter's skill and talent, became a piece of glass and a fragment of the stained-glass window that would later emerge.

The pieces of glass were colored by the use of powders that were derived from plants and minerals by processes that were kept highly secret; they were very often passed on orally and never written down. Even today, the colors of some stained-glass windows cannot be reproduced because we have no clues as to how they were made.

Once they had been colored, the pieces had to be assembled in accordance with the template. Bands of lead were used to hold together the various fragments of the stained-glass window as it began to take shape.

## Installation and Maintenance

Once it had been assembled in the workshop, the stained-glass window was dismantled and transported to the cathedral site. Piece by piece, the glass mosaic was raised and placed into its final position.

As with many other crafts associated with the cathedral, arrangements had to be made for the maintenance of the work. For this reason, a glass artist was often employed to care for the windows. He received a sum that was not inconsiderable for this job: eight livres per year, in the case of the abbey church of Saint-Denis.

The constant need for new windows made the thirteenth century one of the most creative and fertile periods in the history of stained-glass windows. Thanks to the extraordinary skills of the craftsmen and glass artists, these windows provide us with precious testimony about a society that revolved around people who prayed, people who fought, and those who worked. Once appealing primarily to the imagination of believers and pilgrims, these glass paintings still have the power to delight and inspire admiration in all the visitors who take the time to look at them.

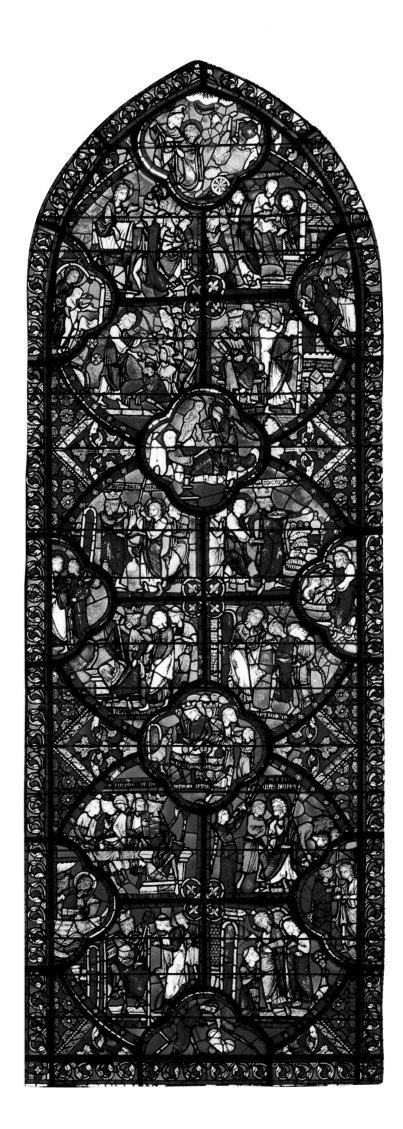

◆ The window of Saint Thomas at the cathedral of Bourges.

♦ The Sainte-Chapelle in Paris. The architect—Jean de Chelles or Pierre de Montreuil?—conceived the church as a reliquary enclosed by sixty-six hundred square feet of stained-glass windows.

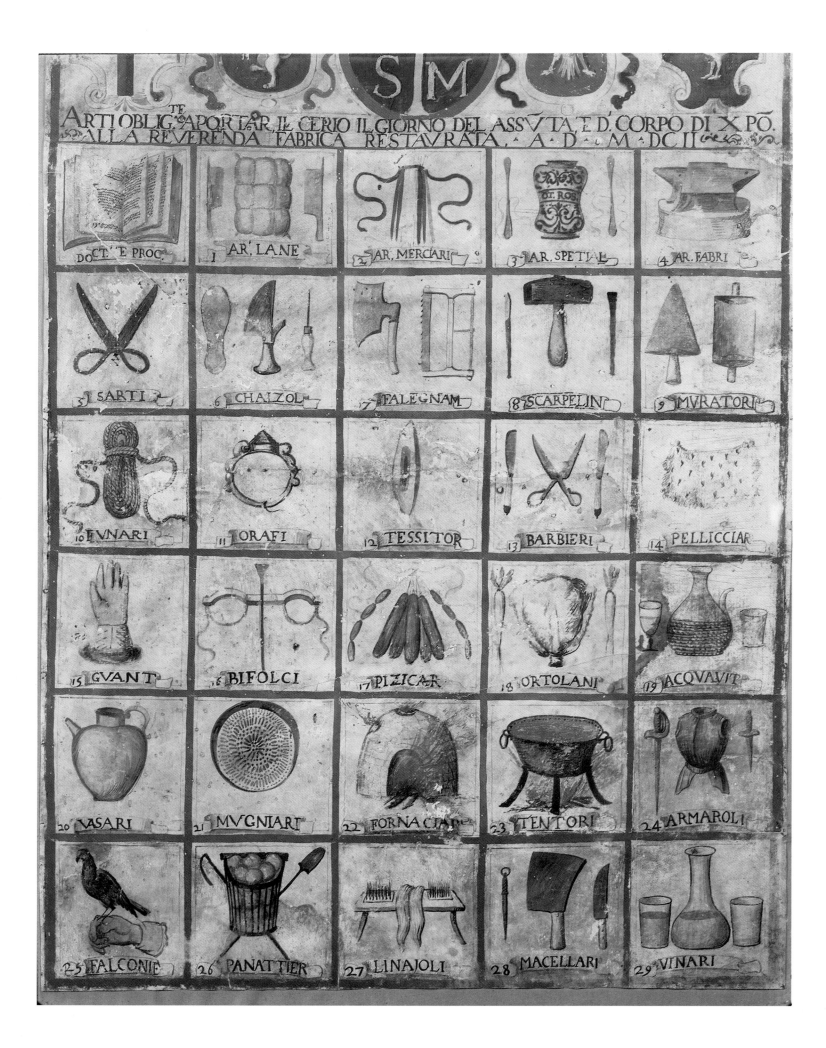

ARTI OBLIG.TE A PORTAR IL CERIO IL GIORNO DEL ASSŪTA E D. CORPO DI XPŌ.
ALLA REVERENDA FABRICA RESTAVRATA · A · D · M · DC II

DOCT. E PROC.

1 AR. LANE

2 AR. MERCIARI

3 AR. SPETIAL

4 AR. FABRI

5 SARTI

6 CHAIZOL

7 FALEGNAM

8 SCARPELIN

9 MVRATORI

10 FVNARI

11 ORAFI

12 TESSITOR

13 BARBIERI

14 PELLICCIAR

15 GVANT

16 BIFOLCI

17 PIZICAR

18 ORTOLANI

19 ACQVAVIT

20 VASARI

21 MVGNIARI

22 FORNACIAR

23 TENTORI

24 ARMAROLI

25 FALCONIE

26 PANATTIER

27 LINAJOLI

28 MACELLARI

29 VINARI

# Other Crafts Associated with the Cathedral Construction-Site

The cathedral was associated with other craftsmen in addition to those that took part in its construction—the carpenters, stonecutters, masons, roofers, plumbers, and glass artists. Less visible on or even absent from the cathedral building-sites, many other craftsmen played an important role in the successful completion of these projects.

In studies on this subject, there is little mention of the teams of unskilled construction workers who were employed in the early stages of the building work to prepare and shape the ground on which the cathedral would stand. Their labor was absolutely essential, and there must have been some clear policy of welcoming, looking after, and supervising these teams of young workers who dug foundations that could be up to seven or eight yards deep, as was the case in Milan. Before one could think of bringing in materials for the building work, contractors had to be hired to oversee the removal of earth and rubble.

We have already stressed the major role played by the transportation of materials. Genuine companies became specialized in the conveyance of stone and wood. The heavy stone had to be moved by road or river, and such haulage was a very profitable business. By consulting the book of expenses from the Autun workshops for the year 1294–95, we can see that the chapter had to pay "four livres, ten sous, and nine deniers for the transportation of the stones that were called 'gargoyles.'" The transportation of wood was always one of the greatest expenses borne by the master of the works, and it was one of his main concerns.

✦ *Opposite:* This table of the corporations of fourteenth-century Orvieto illustrates the economic wealth of a medieval city. Of the crafts represented, almost all are related to the cathedral building-site and the people who worked on it.

The animals that were used in the conveyance of materials—oxen, horses, and mules—also generated essential activities and involved expenses that had to be calculated into the building site's annual operating budget—the shoeing of horses, the manufacture of saddles and collars, the supplying of hay and oats. The list did not end there. Large numbers of carts had to be made, maintained, and repaired. This was the job of the cartwrights.

As discussed above, the building of a cathedral also required scaffolding, arches, and lifting

✦ *Below:* A fifteenth-century miniature showing the dyeing of clothes.

◆ *Right:* Tailors, from a detail of a fresco in the castle of Issogno, Italy.

equipment. Essential in all these cases was the ropemaker, who supplied the carpenters with top-quality ropes. From the makers of the door frames and the makers of the doors, the casters, the bell-makers, and others who have long since been forgotten, such as the drapers and tailors who supplied the fabrics and made the clothing for the architect, the most un-usual trades and the classic ones had to be in-cluded in the budgetary plans so that adequate sums of money could be raised.

Innkeepers and taverners provided room and board for many of the workers on the cathedral sites. Bakers, butchers, and other pro-viders of food were paid directly or indirectly by the workshop committee, which had to see that the workers were adequately fed so that they could labor "loyally and correctly." Individuals who lived close to the cathedral building-site profited by renting out sheds, attics, and stables. The ca-thedral was thus a factor that made the urban economy more dynamic by also employing a range of businesses and workers who had little to do with the actual building trades.

◆ *Opposite:* A meal at an inn, in a detail from a fourteenth-century miniature.

◆ *Left:* The making or repairing of tools led to the development of specialized crafts, such as that of the edge-tool makers. This carpenter's workbench gives an idea of the large number of tools needed by each corporation.

# Some of the Expenses that Appear in the Ledger of the Workshop Committee of Autun for the Year 1294–95 (extracts)

In the quarries, for the extraction of stones destined for the maintenance of the church of Saint-Lazare: 8 livres, 10 sous, 4 deniers

Ditto for lime, for the entire year: 9 livres, 8 sous

For fine timber destined for the arches of the church of Saint-Lazare, for the carpenters and the laborers: 17 livres, 2 sous, 7 deniers

To the forge of Autun, for the year: 42 livres, 10 sous, 6 deniers

To the laborers, for the opening of the said quarry: 4 livres, 15 sous, 4 deniers

For research on the condition of the quarry of Marmontain: 1 livre, 10 sous

For the laborers who lifted the tiles onto the roof of the church of Saint-Lazare: 1 livre, 9 sous, 11 deniers

For the long poles destined for the final boards: 5 sous

For the manufacture and the iron wheels of twelve carts: 1 livre, 15 sous

To the carpenters, for the fine wood prepared in the chapter's forest: 8 livres, 16 sous

For the rebuilding of the roof of the church of Saint-Lazare and the placement of the equipment, to the carpenters and laborers: 3 livres, 15 sous

To the carpenters who fitted the boards on the roof of the church of Saint-Lazare: 10 livres, 8 sous

For the purchase of the boards: 3 sous, 6 deniers

For the nails and other ironwork necessary for the building of the church of Saint-Lazare: 16 sous, 8 deniers

To Master Pierre of Dijon, roofer: 70 livres

Costs relating to the stones known as "gargoyles": 4 livres, 10 sous, 9 deniers

To Renaud, the innkeeper, for the renting of the house where the above-named master is presently living, for two terms of this year: 3 livres

For the clothes of the said master, the coming term of the birth of Saint John the Baptist not included: 10 livres

For the kingpins and the iron nuts: 18 sous, 3 deniers

For the manufacture of the roofer's meshes: 1 sou, 10 deniers

To Benoît the saddler, for the year, for the saddles, collars, floor fastenings, and other leather items relating to the cart: 2 livres, 10 sous

For the hay, for the harnesses of the said cart: 19 livres, 17 sous, 4 deniers

For oats: 25 livres, 3 sous, 9 deniers

For horseshoes for the horses: 4 livres, 6 sous

For the iron and nails used to strengthen the carts and to repair old ones: 6 livres, 9 sous, 1 denier

To the cartwright, for the new carts and the repair of the old ones: 2 livres, 14 sous, 9 deniers

For melted tallow, oil, vinegar, and thirty pounds of candles, for the year: 2 livres, 7 sous

For the renting, expenses, and loading of the cart: 18 livres

For the renting of sheds, stables, and lofts: 2 livres

For the ropes: 13 deniers

To look after a horse: 5 sous

For the purchase of a horse for the cart: 3 livres, 10 sous

# VI  THE MEMORY
## OF THE BUILDERS

# Memory and History

✦ *Above:* Figure studies and an architectural sketch from the book of drawings of Villard de Honnecourt.

✦ *Right:* The seated Christ, from the sketchbook of Villard de Honnecourt.

✦ *Page 144:* Plan drawn in 1250–60 for the facade of Notre-Dame in Strasbourg. This drawing on parchment is preserved in the Museum of the Oeuvre Notre-Dame de Strasbourg, which holds one of the richest collections of tracings and working drawings. The oldest date to the middle of the thirteenth century.

✦ *Page 145:* Detail of workers from a miniature from *La Fleur des histoires.*

In contrast to history, which is a reconstruction of what no longer is, and which is always problematic, memory seems to be synonymous with life because it is carried by individuals and groups of people, who give it a symbolic dimension that is relevant to present-day reality. But because of this, memory, which is always evolving, is open to the dual processes of remembering and forgetting, and therefore appears extremely vulnerable to any use or misuse.

Unlike history, which aims to be an intellectual and rational process requiring analysis and criticism, memory is much more subjective and emotional, and only retains those elements that reassure it, thereby authorizing any number of acts of censorship that may be deliberate or involuntary. By placing both precise and vague recollections into the domain of the sacred, memory has as one of its purposes to cement together a social group by giving it a kind of absolute truth that history cannot guarantee.

If the world of the cathedrals has its history, one that is always problematic and incomplete, it also has a memory. That memory is both collective and individual, and it varies in relation to the schools, groups, and individuals wishing to claim it to varying degrees and for various purposes. Texts, objects, images, and places of memory thus work together to create an imaginary world of the cathedral that is in a continuous process of being constructed. The historian must sort out the truth by distinguishing the essential from what is secondary, while knowing that his or her modest endeavors will carry little weight by comparison with a realm of the imagination that prefers to see the cathedral as a starting point for all kinds of conjectures, including those that are quite probable and those that appear to be most unreal.

The same is true for the texts, documents, places, and institutions that we have chosen to present below. From the *Regius* Manuscript to the Statutes of Strasbourg, from Villard de Honnecourt to the Companions of the Tour of France, many readings are possible in the attempt to ascertain whether the world of the builders has been evoked with more or less accuracy in these documents.

On this occasion, the historian has deliberately decided not to present his own analysis and critique in a systematic way. Instead, readers are free to make their way between history and memory and to decide what belongs to the real world of the cathedrals and to their own imagination.

# The Book of Drawings of Villard de Honnecourt

*Villard de Honnecourt greets you and asks all those who are working on the various kinds of projects that are contained in this book to pray for his soul and to remember him; in this book, you can find much help and advice on the principles of building in stone and on the construction of wooden frameworks. You will also find in it advice on the techniques of portraiture and drawing, as they are taught and required by the principles of geometry.*

Villard de Honnecourt's book of drawings has to-day achieved the status of a major reference work for any study of the art, architecture, sciences, and associated techniques of the early thirteenth century. It is according to some people an account of the work of a construction site, and according to others it is a book of notes. Many questions exist about the author. An architect, engineer, artist, and teacher—who, in fact, was Villard, the man who was born in a small village in Picardy called Honnecourt? The answers to these queries remain unclear.

His book of drawings, or sketchbook—at least what is left of it—is now famous because some of the plates have been reproduced in a large number of specialized and more general publications. Master Villard's sketchbook is a very important document in the history of the techniques of certain crafts in the thirteenth century, particularly those of the masons, carpenters, stonecutters, and other artists who worked on the medieval building-sites. The world of the cathedrals comes back to life through this extraordinary document of thirty-three folios, both sides of which are covered with text and drawings. According to Hans R. Hahnloser, it was

♦ "It is an entire world that one sees coming back to life in this sketchbook; a world that builds and what it builds is meant to last for a very long time, because it is passionate about solid materials and a just balance." Régine Pernoud.

♦ *Right:* The Church, as seen by Villard de Honnecourt.

♦ *Below:* From left to right, a goat-headed demon; a snail; a study of the head of a man; a heraldic eagle.

◆ Villard's drawings are the fruit of his travels: "I have been to many lands," he wrote in his sketchbook.

to have contained sixty-two folios. Today the remains of the original sketchbook are housed in the Bibliothèque Nationale de France, in Paris.

From the erection of Reims Cathedral to the labyrinth at Chartres, and including the towers of Laon Cathedral and the reproduction of ingenious systems such as the hydraulic saw (whose mechanism he did not understand), Villard captured, by means of the pen and pencil, great monuments and their builders as he himself saw them. He traveled from one building site to the next, recording what he observed; he also copied documents he had been supplied with, principally projects that had been abandoned by their architects.

A talented artist and draftsman as well as a technician who was especially interested in the practice of making working drawings, Villard was above all a witness who enables us to get to know the Middle Ages, which can always be discovered anew and in an original way. It is not impossible or fanciful to think that Villard may, from time to time, have acted as a consultant to architects who wished to define a project on the basis of several different sets of drawings. Yet this is only one further hypothesis in our search for the true identity of Villard de Honnecourt.

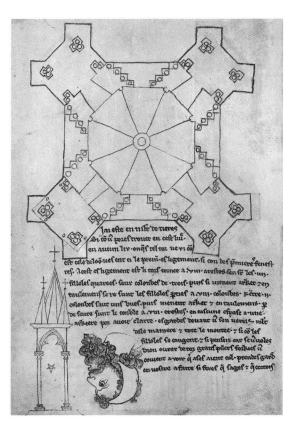

His sketchbook is therefore an irreplaceable document, which was written and drawn at the very moment when Europe was experiencing an unprecedented architectural boom. In spite of a number of imperfections, we cannot fail to admire his achievement when we study the folios, such as the one that shows the technique employed to verify, by means of sightings from the ground, the balance of a keystone in a vault that was forty yards high.

We should also note that in his sketchbook Villard appears as a genius inventor, a kind of French Leonardo da Vinci, to borrow a comparison some specialists have used. Besides the hydraulic saw, Villard draws a war machine, a jack, a portable hand-warmer, a mechanical bird . . .

We shall not present here a complete study of a book that has already been extensively examined by such eminent experts as Alain Erlande-Brandenburg, Roland Bechmann, Régine Pernoud, and Jean Gimpel. Readers are referred to the fascinating book *Carnet de Villard de Honnecourt, 13ème siècle* (The Sketchbook of Villard de Honnecourt, 13th century), which reproduces the entire sketchbook and provides comprehensive analyses of the author and his work.

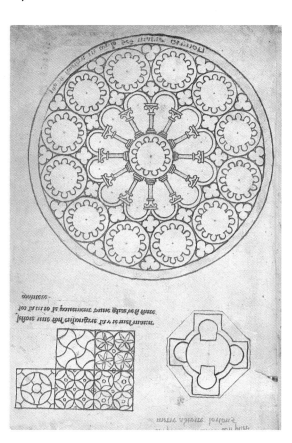

◆ *Right:* Drawing of the western rose window of Chartres.

◆ *Opposite:* Villard simplified his drawings to emphasize the characteristics of the subject that interested him the most.

# The Museum of the Oeuvre
# Notre-Dame de Strasbourg

Created in 1206 with the aim of overseeing the construction and decoration of the cathedral of Strasbourg, the Oeuvre Notre-Dame's initial objective was to collect donations and bequests destined for the cathedral. The finances were administered jointly by the bishop and the chapter until 1262, when the chapter gained exclusive control over the administration of the workshops' revenues.

In 1290, the workshops passed into the hands of the city council, which was anxious that the revenues be better administered so that work on the building site not be interrupted. The transfer of responsibility took place while Erwin von Steinbach was the master of the works. The Oeuvre Notre-Dame definitively became a municipal organization while fully retaining its specific identity, since it alone had responsibility for the building site and its financing. During the French Revolution, the Oeuvre Notre-Dame, which was considered a church workshop, was placed under the direction of the State Property Department; it was handed back to the city in 1803.

The present museum of the Oeuvre Notre-Dame is housed in a building erected in 1347 on the site of the Maison de l'Oeuvre, which was built in 1274. It is made up of a medieval wing and a Renaissance wing, which housed the lodge of the stonecutters (which was to become the Grand Lodge of the German Empire in 1459). The first lodge was located in the southeast corner of the

♦ *Left:* The Defeated Synagogue. Blindfolded, she holds a broken lance and the tablets of the Law. In her vanquished state, she remains beautiful and noble.

medieval wing, which was destroyed, with the exception of the arch around the door, by the bombing raids of 1944.

The forty-two rooms that make up this exceptionally fine museum offer a complex but coherent journey for visitors, who may examine statues, stained-glass windows, corporation chests, plans, working drawings, and even the greatly admired stonecutters' lodge itself.

The Oeuvre Notre-Dame also houses an important archive, most notably, the account books of the workshops, as well as charters, bequests, gifts, and municipal and church documents dating

from the thirteenth to the end of the fifteenth century. With the plans, working drawings, and associated sketches, these documents form a precious body of texts that sheds much valuable light on the way in which the construction site operated and was financed, and on its technical aspects and everyday functioning, focusing on the specific example of Strasbourg Cathedral.

The Oeuvre Notre-Dame contains, in particular, one of the very few collections of plans and drawings on parchment still in existence. Especially noteworthy are the earliest large plans relating to the cathedral's western facade. The plans for the towers, the spire, and the narthex were realized with the same objective in mind: to give the decision makers and the financiers a picture, even if it was not to scale, of the work that was envisaged. In the majority of cases, these were elevation drawings rather than plans. It should be noted that several plans or proposals relating to Strasbourg Cathedral are preserved in other cities, including Bern, London, and Vienna, a fact that provides additional proof of the importance of Strasbourg in the medieval "catalogue" that circulated among architects and masters of the works in medieval Europe.

✦ *Left:* Saints Mary Magdalen and Catherine, as portrayed by Konrad Witz in the fifteenth century.

✦ *Right:* The tempter presents the attitudes of the initiate: feet and right arm at right angles. But behind him appear frogs, toads, and entwined serpents. The apple may symbolize the forbidden fruit, but the tempter does not present a completely negative impression, and invites us to overcome our passions.

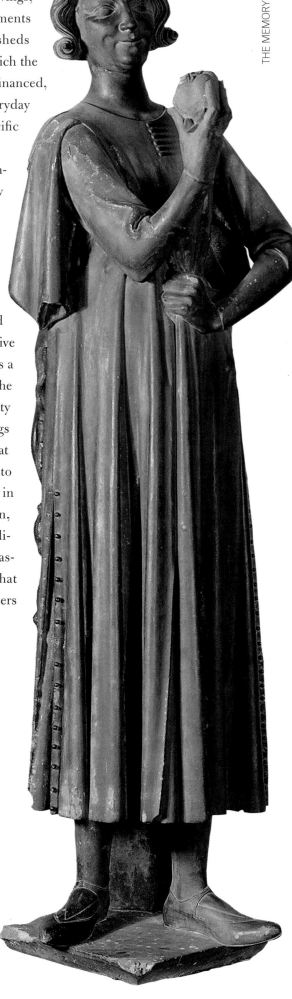

# The Companions of the Tour of France

### The Successors of the Cathedral Builders?

At the dawn of the twenty-first century, two beliefs are commonly held about the Companions of the Tour of France. The first is that they are systematically associated with the "makers of fine works": they create artistic masterpieces, possess a love of work that is well done, are committed to the pursuit of quality, and have a professional conscience. The second is that they are considered by most people to be the true successors or descendants of the cathedral builders.

We shall not repeat here an interpretation that this historian presented in a previous study (*La France des Compagnons* [France of the companions]), in order to define the complex identity of a French association of companions, or journeymen craftsmen, that was able to last through the centuries by successfully balancing the relative importance of the concepts of tradition and modernity.

The Union compagnonnique des compagnons du Tour de France des devoirs unis, the Association ouvrière des compagnons du devoir du Tour de France, and the Fédération compagnonnique des métiers du bâtiment, which are the three organizations that make up the world of the

craftsmen's guilds and associations in present-day France, are the rightful heirs of the ancient journeymen's associations that emerged in the last two centuries of the Middle Ages. But even if this is the case, with what degree of certainty may the Companions of the Tour of France be regarded as the true heirs and successors of the cathedral builders? That is the principal question that has inspired the present study.

### On the Need to Find Accurate Information

The great French medievalists who have studied the special world of the cathedral builders are careful not to state with certainty that the origins of the associations of companions lie clearly in the realm of the Gothic cathedral. In addition to the confusion that may arise because of the problem of vocabulary (a companion of the corporation suggests a nonitinerant worker; a companion of the Tour of France implies an itinerant one), it is always difficult for historians of the associations of companions to prove that they were attached to the cathedrals, even though it is very probable that it was from the cathedral building-sites that groups of workers gradually emerged, seeking the freedom to travel as an essential means of gaining training and promotion.

It is clear, today, that the cathedral building-site was a special crossroads, where nonitinerant and traveling workers toiled side by side. The former (who were often tied to a corporation in the city) discovered, through the example of the latter, the great privilege that it was to have the freedom to move around from one building site and from

✦ In the thirteenth century, many Bibles included illustrations of the building or the rebuilding of the Temple of Jerusalem. These were based on observations the artists made on the cathedral construction-site.

✦ *Pages 152–53:* Strasbourg Cathedral, a marvel in stone.

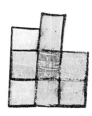

one city to another. It should be remembered that French companions' associations were initially structured in a clandestine way by the first rebellious companions who challenged a system of corporations that they considered too unjust and too restrictive. It was those first courageous and bold craftsmen, who dared to defy the corporations, who would lay the foundations of a new form of guild that was freed from the authority of the masters who were increasingly restricting admission to the title of master to their own sons or sons-in-law. But the historical picture cannot be reduced to this simple image. All the crafts were not involved at the same time or in the same way.

It is, nevertheless, important to point out

# The Point of View of a Companion Stonecutter of the *Devoir* (Duty Guild)

The builders of the cathedrals were coming together in workshops when the concepts of the artists and architect as we understand them today had still not been developed. In fact, the whole corporation came together there, including the manager of the building site, the architect, who was simply a mason, stonecutter, or carpenter (the engineers of their day), and even the lowly mortar-mixer. Neither should we forget the artists who had not yet left in search of fame and prestige. We recall the well-known portrayal of these people by Fouquet, in his amazing miniature painting of the building of the Temple. There we see, united fraternally by their work, the man who is sculpting a statue, the one in charge of the machinery, and the one who is preparing quicklime. That was companionship in action; the best people did not run away, and the humble and less-privileged workers labored just as effectively for the glory of the project as those who had been specially commissioned. These expert craftsmen sustained the community by their zeal and translated the faith of all into works of which everyone felt proud. The age of companionship still marks us profoundly. Do we not call ourselves the sons of the cathedral builders? It is in this respect that we are the guardians of the secret of working people's souls.

—J. Bernard, *Compagnonnage*

✦ *Above:* Nineteenth-century members of the Association ouvrière des compagnons du devoir du Tour de France—the Companions of the Tour of France—take vows in a ceremony with medieval roots.

✦ *Left:* As is evident in this miniature from *La Fleur des histoires,* many artists copied the model of Jean Fouquet (see page 52).

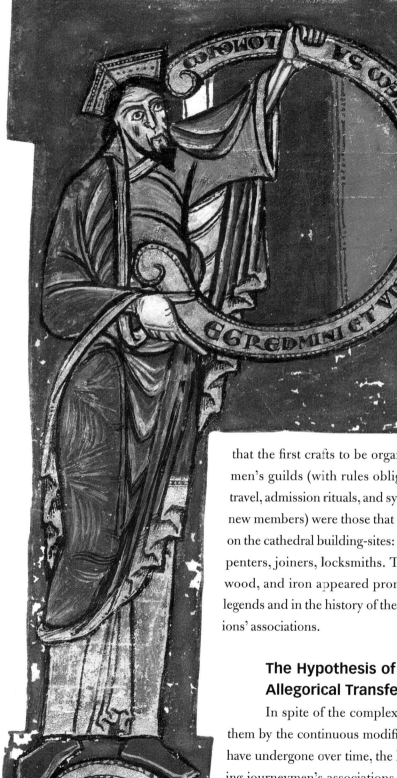

that the first crafts to be organized into craftsmen's guilds (with rules obliging members to travel, admission rituals, and symbolic names for new members) were those that were represented on the cathedral building-sites: stonecutters, carpenters, joiners, locksmiths. The trio of stone, wood, and iron appeared prominently, both in legends and in the history of the French companions' associations.

## The Hypothesis of Allegorical Transfer

In spite of the complexity conferred on them by the continuous modifications that they have undergone over time, the legends concerning journeymen's associations rapidly gave rise to the transformation of the extraordinary medieval building-site that surrounded the emerging cathedral into an ideal and symbolic building-site around the masterpiece being constructed, which was itself symbolized by the Temple of Jerusalem. The large number of workers, the necessary organization and hierarchy of skills and of those workers (apprentices, companions, masters), and the putting into place of distinctive signs were all incorporated into legends that quite simply trans-

◆ Solomon, the son of David, represented in an initial letter in a twelfth-century Bible.

ferred the cathedral building-site to the building site of Jerusalem. This was much more sacred and much more grandiose in the minds of the people of the Middle Ages, whether they were cultivated or uneducated. We think of medieval miniatures, which illustrated such details as the various colors denoting the different crafts, or signs expressed in clothing, for example, apprentices shown wearing knee-length stockings.

It would be wrong and even ridiculous to claim that as early as the thirteenth century, legends were being formed that still control the symbolism and heritage of French craftsmen's associations in our own time. This process took place gradually by means of successive additions and modifications, which made of the guilds' legends an entire system. It was a complex but coherent system from the moment the method of interpretation began to take into account the medieval universe, which was the first key to accurately understanding the slow elaboration of the identity of the guilds in France.

The three legendary founding fathers of those craftsmen's organizations, King Solomon, Master Jacques (a knight), and Father Soubise (a monk), appear in the medieval origins of a society of companion builders who worked in response to commissions that they received from powerful individuals (Solomon), with the protection of military orders during their travels, especially during the Crusades (Jacques), and with the help of the spiritual and professional support that was given to them by some monastic orders (Soubise). Here, again, we should not be satisfied with our first impression. The three founders of journeymen's associations were also bearers of other messages that were more or less logical and coherent. Jacques, the stonecutter, and Father Soubise, an expert in carpentry, recall the predominance of these two professions, which were so essential to the building of a cathedral. Father Soubise highlights the virtues and values of the life of the companions' community, which though it was not necessarily monastic did respect the observance of one monastic rule as it sought to protect the interest and cohesion of the group. The legends cannot thus be read and interpreted as representing certainties that were established once and for all. A series of hypotheses formed around them, which vary in relation to the social group that is considering the significance and history of the cathedrals.

In fact, it is very important to look carefully at the miniatures painted by Jean Fouquet and by his contemporaries when we want to understand the importance of Jerusalem to the medieval and postmedieval mind. The most famous painting, as mentioned above, shows the building of a cathedral by a symbolic transfer that aims to present the Gothic building as the symbolic model of the heavenly Jerusalem. What presents itself as an illustration of the Temple of Jerusalem is nothing more than a depiction of the cathedral building-site of the thirteenth century.

The French craftsmen's guilds and associations of today, as the successors of the workers' communities that recommended travel from as early as the thirteenth century, are logically the guardians of a body of legends and myths that were built up by the accumulation of memories and details relating to a cathedral construction-site that left a clear mark on the minds of the masters and workers. In 1268, the provost of Paris, Etienne Boileau, presented his *Livres des metiers* to the king, with the aim of putting some sort of order into the professions that were still referred to as "wild."

Here we are delving into the heart of the duality that pits history against memory. Although we cannot officially prove a close connection between the companions of today and the builders of yesterday, it is nonetheless true to say that the Companions of the Tour of France can unquestionably call themselves the successors of the cathedral builders. The written texts produced by the three French associations of companion journeymen do, in fact, make these connections.

LE PÈRE SOUBISE
de Maitre Jacques Fondateur des Compagnons passants Charpentiers du Devoir des Couvreurs et des Platre...

◆ Father Soubise, one of the three legendary founders of the craftsmen's guilds.

◆ *Pages 158–59:* This nineteenth-century image by Leclair Picqueur depicts the promotion ceremony of a companion carpenter in the Duty Guild who has completed his tour of France.

# Freemasonry

An institution that had its origins in the founding of the Grand Lodge of London in 1717, Freemasonry can barely prove that it has existed for three centuries. However, in spite of this historical reality, many Freemasons still like to consider themselves the rightful heirs of the cathedral builders.

The vocabulary (lodge, apprentice, companion, master) and symbolic objects (the trowel, level, perpendicular, square, and dividers) that are used were indeed borrowed from the medieval builders. But Freemasons do not actually take part in building projects. The medieval heritage is thus transferred from the realm of function to that of symbol in the context of an intellectual process that appeals to the world of the builders as it searches for a basis upon which to formulate its reflections.

Legends and myths, such as that of the Temple of Jerusalem, which is also referred to in Freemasonry, only act as modules to be used in the construction of the temple of humanity, a very complicated project whose definition may vary, depending on each organization or even each individual who engages in it.

The historian has to make it clear that in order to construct its own identity Freemasonry drew on various sources: on the Bible, the Cabala, alchemy, but also on the Templars and the Rosicrucians. It was an inclusive and open system, within which the cathedral and the world of its builders were only elements of a Masonic symbolism that borrowed parts of various movements and ideas as it was being constituted. Each of them contributed to the definition of a tradition that can differ significantly from one variant to another.

In this way, the workers and lodges of the cathedrals provide the intellectual society of Freemasonry with an aura of earlier history that history itself cannot rightfully give it because of the absence of clear evidence. That fact is underlined by Luc Nefontaine, one of the greatest French experts on the history of Freemasonry. Lacking proof of its historical origins, Freemasonry seeks a mythical connection with and origin in the cathedral builders, of whose memory it wishes to be the guardian. However, this is yet another area in which memory should not be confused with history.

◆ A Freemason in formal dress, pictured in an engraving made in 1735.

# The Guild of the Masons

**A**ll the medieval documents tell us that masons gathered in lodges, buildings that were located next to the building sites. There they passed on the secrets of their crafts, under the authority of the master mason, who trained and supported the apprentices. Young men remained apprentices for several years before they had acquired enough experience to be recognized as companions. Brothers had to be loyal, respectful, honest, and conscientious in their work, otherwise they risked being excluded from the guild of masons. If there were initiations, they consisted merely in the passing on of technical skills, and not in a symbolic ceremony that formally made the candidate a member of a group of masons by means of a precise ritual. In this context, there was absolutely no question of anyone being nominated; professional competence alone was the determining factor.

—Luc Nefontaine,
*La Franc-maçonnerie,*
*une fraternité dévoilée*

✦ *Above:* Elements represented on a Masonic apron,
from an engraving of 1826.

# The Texts

## The *Regius* Manuscript

The *Regius* Manuscript is a poem consisting of 794 octosyllabic lines written in Middle English, the medieval language of southwestern England in 1390. It appears to be the work of an expert, possibly of an architect, who was very familiar with the builders' traditions. Composed with the aims of unifying disparate statutes, commenting on morals and customs that were influenced by Gallo-Roman traditions, and protecting the interests of the patrons and architects and of their teams, the *Regius* is still an active participant in the ongoing debate among historians of the builders' associations.

The *Regius* Manuscript consists of several distinct parts:

1. A history (or, rather, a legendary account) of the profession of the builder
2. Fifteen articles that explicitly define the statutes to be observed
3. A supplement to the statutes, divided into fifteen points
4. Several other provisions and decisions
5. The legend of the Four Crowned Men
6. The Tower of Babel
7. The seven liberal arts that were to be taught
8. The duty of attending mass and of observing the rituals
9. A treatise of good manners to be observed

───────────────❋───────────────

We shall reproduce here only points 2 and 3, which relate to the context that has been studied in this book. They provide ample evidence of the manner in which the free professions were organized in fourteenth-century England.

Those wishing to read the entire *Regius* may refer to the excellent study by René Dez, Regius, *manuscrit 1390, première lueur de l'aube au pied des cathédrales, la charte la plus ancienne des franc-mestiers de bâtisseurs.*

### ✵ *Here begins the First article*

Article one: Geometry
The Master mason shall be
loyal to his brotherhood.
He shall never require of the companion
any more than he can do.
In good faith he will set his just salary
at the cost of living.
Master mason, here is your law:
Always act as an honest boss;
may nobody await in vain
this rigor that you are praised for.
Never accept a pot of wine [a bribe]
from a companion, and do not receive
from your Lord anything of any sort
coming from the worst or the best
that dignity cannot bear.
Thus, with no reticence,
your conscience will be untroubled.

### ✵ *Second article*

Article two: Masonry
Every Master owes to his function
to be present at his congregation
without ever, through carelessness,
omitting to observe
this strict obligation.
He should therefore be informed
of the exact location of the meeting
which the Assembly will have decided.
Unless he has a valid excuse,
the absent Master will be charged
with disobedience or guile.
Sickness, when it occurs,
will be the only reason for his absence.

### ✵ *Third article*

Article three: the Master shall not accept
an apprentice for longer than seven years.
Having to teach him his principles,
he will hire him for that long.
A shorter course is without benefit
to the Lord, to the student, or to the
Master.
A shorter period is not sufficient
for the rules of the art that he has to
transmit.

### ✵ *Fourth article*

Article four goes like this:
Whoever he may have approached,
the Master should not, even with respect,
take a serf as an apprentice
or hire him out of avarice.
For the Lord may at any moment
seek him out to serve Him
and take him away, one knows how.
If he appeared in a lodge
the Master would take great care of him.
He who goes against this point
may suffer because of this, as may
his companions, who are all together.
Every mason should be well born
to receive, as they appear, the secrets
given to him.
In an old charter, for this purpose,
this noble adage is inscribed:
"Take an apprentice more highly placed,
and teach him your craft."

### ✵ *Fifth article*

Article five states, justly and wisely,
May the apprentice be of pure blood.
Thus the Master who hires him
must make certain that he feels
neither trouble, nor any serious wound,
that he is not deformed or that his body
is not mutilated, that his walk
is not that of a lame person, or that he
has to walk like an invalid
and not bear any great effort.
A mason cannot lose face;
his trade requires strong men.
It would do him great harm
to ignore this privilege.

### ✵ *Sixth article*

Article six cannot displease
him who is devoted to his Lord.
He cannot even pay
a salary to any aide except the best.
The companion who is perfect in his art
would not wish to see himself
paid the same amount
as the apprentice who progresses

by small steps, but holds
only very few of the Master's secrets.
Day after day knowledge comes to him,
but he is far from knowing all.
Therefore his wages shall be raised
while he pursues his course
and as his skills grow.
One day the rewards will be his.

### ✵ *Seventh article*

Article seven deserves to be studied:
A Master shall never give shelter,
out of fear or concern,
to thieves, brigands, or rogues,
persons of ill repute.
Giving clothes, food, and lodging to
the underworld
would do harm to the corporation,
whose honor it is to be honest.

### ✵ *Eighth article*

Article eight is very useful:
When a mason has not been able
to go from being an ignorant to being
a skilled man,
the Master may replace him
with someone who is better at his work.
The clumsiness of the weaker one
might do great damage
to the image of his profession.

### ✵ *Ninth article*

Article nine requires that the Master
shall have the resources and the authority
to which each person should submit,
since he has merited such a position
from his Lord.
He shall plan solidly
the structures of the building
and shall care for its foundations.

### ✵ *Tenth article*

Article ten states that no Master
or companion of this profession
shall ever allow himself
to take the place on the building site
of another worker, who precedes him,

for all masons, like brothers and sisters,
should unite, offer each other their help,
and never supplant one of their own.
Every worker has the right to live.
The punishment is severe for anyone
who commits
such a crime: ten good livres,
and the mark of shame forever.
However, when the work undertaken
by ignorance or bad workmanship
is compromised and presents a danger,
if the Lord sends a mason
to work to rebuild it,
he can agree to do it,
his skills being required,
without fearing any ambiguity.
But on every other occasion,
a mason who received a firm contract,
who builds the foundations,
must complete his work alone.

### ✸ Eleventh article

This good article, one can say,
has as its sole object to forbid
the mason to do any work in the evening
or night, except for practice,
to progress in his knowledge.
He would get no benefit from it.

### ✸ Twelfth article

You must not blame another's work,
whether he is a brother in your lodge
or not.
Let honest praise be known,
of his work, without embarrassment.
To preserve your own honor,
make his talent appear even better.
In your praise lies his happiness.
It is by doing this that one collaborates.

### ✸ Thirteenth article

Article thirteen teaches the Master,
who is hiring an apprentice,
that he should make everything known
of the art whose slightest detail
he has consented to reveal.
The pupil will make this his store of
knowledge.

### ✸ Fourteenth article

And this article is one of the wisest,
which gives the Master the obligation
of not offering an apprenticeship
unless he can fulfill the condition
of varying by his work
all the aspects of the profession.

### ✸ Fifteenth article

Article fifteen, for what it is worth,
puts its accent on honesty,
and decency, that true cement
binding the Master to his team.
To proscribe false oaths among them
shall be their very first principle.
They will thus preserve their souls
from vice and enmity.
They will thus avoid rebukes,
to the great honor of their profession.

✦ The building of the Tower of Babel,
in a drawing after a twelfth-century
illuminated manuscript.

## Supplement to the Statutes:

It is fitting to include
in these statutes the supplement
that was established by the Lords and
Masters:
Whoever takes building as his profession
must love God and His Church,
his companions, and also his Master.
On all building sites, he must tell
himself this,
and must behave accordingly.

### Second point

The second point, in its terms,
tells the Master: work your week,
to deserve your pay and rest.
Do not begrudge effort and trouble,
work that is well done makes a person
happy,
for in it does he find his reward.

### Third point

From the very strict third point,
the apprentice should not omit
to learn this lesson:
Whatever is said in a lodge
is the secret of every mason:
The Master's words, advice, praise,
criticism, too, rules of the art,
debates in a large or small room
should never, by chance,
leave the circle of its members.
Observe the law of silence,
for your honor, do not waver.

### Fourth point

The statute says in point four:
Be faithful to the people of the profession,
even if you have to fight for them
think, masons, that you were
nothing before you were admitted by those
whose apprentice, dumb with fear,
receives at the cost of his submission
the most precious pieces of advice.

### Fifth point

Point five has prescribed this:

A mason, receiving his salary,
the sum justly owed him, says thank you
very much
to the person employing him, who is
content
not to reproach him for any offense.
But the Master, in good justice,
should inform him before noon
if he does not want his services anymore.
If a mason gets such an order,
he must not start any debate.

### Sixth point

If it happens that a conflict divides,
at any level, high or low,
one brother from another and that discord
too seriously arises between them,
point six states that in
this rare and unfortunate case,
an interview shall be granted to the
opponents,
at which the conciliating mason
will be able to show its author
what blunder he has committed
and shall restore peace.
By a statement of true quality,
the Master, in his love of God,
shall let the Law speak,
holding counsel outside of work,
during the evening hours.

### Seventh point

The seventh point extols in detail
all the most moral virtues
in order to live to old age in the Christian
faith:
Never take another man's wife.
Take care not to make your own
the Master's or the person's who
works with you every day.
Would you like to lose your wife?
Respect the other person under his roof.
Whoever would commit such a vile act,
exposing himself to the constant scorn
of all masons, for this outrage,
should be condemned to go back
into apprenticeship for seven years.

### Eighth point

Point eight is expressed in this way:
the most skilfull companion
who has received the esteem of the Master,
for having shown himself worthy of the
right
to supervise as a responsible man
the good progress of the work,
must always be just
toward everyone, for what that is worth.

### Ninth point

Ninth, after the previous one,
this point states the prerogatives
and the duties of the intendant,
steward, toward his guests,
when the meal is prepared
in the great refectory hall:
Every companion must be treated
as a brother or sister by the intendant.
Every week the person occupying this role
will be changed.
Nobody will be able to avoid it,
when his time to serve comes around.
Mason, if this responsibility is yours,
take care to pay punctually
every supplier, so that he does not come
to contest that he has been properly paid.
Your companions would be sorry
that on this account their honesty
was being doubted. Everybody must be
able to see
the evidence of the just costs, clearly
stated,
of being fed, knowing very well what it
costs.
May the horrible name of miser
never be attached to you.
Everybody has the right to see the
accounts
of the food of which he had his share.
To do anyone a disservice would be your
shame.
Never raise a rampart
between your brother and your
management.
Be strict and clear, remember this.

### Tenth point

This point answers the question:
How to act, whatever may happen?
When a mason has lowered himself
to vice and when everything accuses
him of this,
to the point that his work is shoddy,
if he looks for a bad excuse
by calumny toward his peers,
causing the greatest harm
to their profession, when it appears
that he is lying. Do not assist him in
his turpitude by helping him;
you would be giving up all respect
for your name, and such an attitude
might also render you suspect.
It is fitting that he be summoned,
according to the law, to appear,
before the council of the lodge,
made up of companions and of their
Master.
If, like a coward, he refuses to go,
he will be expelled by his peers,
for it is stated in the oldest regulations
that he be repudiated.

### Eleventh point

Point eleven, with great wisdom,
tells the mason, when it appears
that a companion of little skill
lacks the advice of an expert Master,
that he should guide him in his work.
He should teach him to make the best use
of his tool, to cut the stone better and
to produce better blocks.
"Show him how to go about it,
be charitable in your advice,
by God, if he knows how to understand
you,
reveal your art to him."

### Twelfth point

Every man of the profession
of builders owes his presence
to the great assembly, whose mission
is to apply its competency

to the interests of this profession.
All the masons who are present in it,
establish in their entirety
rules which all approve before Lords
sheriff and mayor,
all aldermen, and nobles.
No mason may exempt himself from it,
or challenge the established order,
without incurring the penalty of arrest
and the most severe judgment.

### Thirteenth point

Everyone should show an interest
in this point, which reveals itself
to be useful to morality.
He must swear that he will not steal.
He could not profit from theft without
doing mortal injury to his own people.

### Fourteenth point

Point fourteen is inserted here:
Every mason swears the oath with great
respect,
to his Lord, to be faithful to all
aspects of the traditions, rules, and Law,
which everyone in his profession reveres,
companions, Master, in the name of
the King,

and whose excellence is apparent to all.
His actions must always be guided
by the need to conform to every one of
its points.
He will not be tempted to
disobey any of them or
to break the pact that
ties him to all the free masons
by the oath that everybody swears
before his peers. Nobody
shall allow such an omission and
everyone will denounce it.
All are required to examine their skills
strictly.
Whoever refuses or fails to do his duty
shall be brought before the Assembly.

### Fifteenth point

This last point has the merit
of punishing severely
any mason who betrays his oath,
by an order thus transcribed,
which the Assembly has examined,
after fair consultation,
and then stated out loud at its meeting,
which is mentioned above.
If such a fault is proved
against a mason, which the offender
has acknowledged but which he
refuses to make good,
he will be expelled from the profession
that was his, by the Masters.
Held in contempt by all for his treachery,
he will himself have broken the tie
that attached him to that profession.
He will be forbidden to exercise it
ever again, under the penalty that justice
will intervene to punish him;
he will be locked up in a narrow cell
and kept incarcerated;
his assets and his savings will be seized,
for as long as will please the King.

✦ *Opposite:* Bourges Cathedral, a light in the night.

✦ *Left:* Illustration from the *Regius* Manuscript.

## From the Statutes of Ratisbon to the Statutes of Saint Michael

In April 1459, under the presidency of the architect Jost Dotzinger, master of the works of Strasbourg Cathedral, the master stonecutters, who had come from all parts of Europe, gathered in the city of Ratisbon. Their main objective was to unify the statutes of their respective lodges.

After several preparatory meetings, a definitive text was approved by the assembly of master stonecutters. These were the famous Statutes of Ratisbon, which described in detail the organization and daily life of the lodges, hereafter placed under the authority of four main lodges: those of Strasbourg, Cologne, Vienna, and Rome. Strasbourg was elevated to the rank of Grand Lodge and was given the power of final judgment and preeminent authority.

The articles that follow are of great interest because they illustrate, better than any historical study, the attempt that was made to establish a harmonious organization of professional people. The practice of this profession, the relations between masters, companions, and apprentices, and the life of the lodge were all the object of precise articles that describe the daily life of the cathedral builders and reveal a clear concern for detail.

The Statutes of Ratisbon were approved by Emperor Maximilian in 1498. They were revised in 1563, giving birth to a text that was just as important in its approach to the organization and the regulations in force in the communities of builders; it was known as the Statutes of Saint Michael.

◆ The patron and his court pay a visit to the master of the works. From a 1507 Austrian painting depicting the building of the monastery of Klosterneuberg.

## THE STATUTES OF RATISBON
### (Extracts)

*In the name of the Father, Son, and Holy Ghost, and of Holy Mary, Mother of God, of His blessed saints and servants, the Four Crowned Saints, of eternal memory, we believe that, in order to preserve friendship, union, and obedience, the foundation of all good, of all utility, and of benefit to all, princes, counts, lords, buildings, and convents, which are now and shall in the future become churches, buildings made of stone, or constructions, we must form a fraternal community, for the good and benefit of all masters and companions, in the profession of stoneworkers and masons, on German soil, above all in order to avoid any discussion, failure, worry, expenses, and damages that may result from disorderly action and transgressions of our good rules. We pledge that we will institute all the regulations peacefully and amicably. In order that our Christian undertaking may be valid in all ages, we, the masters and companions of the said profession, who come from Speyer, Strasbourg, and Ratisbon, in our own name and in the name of all the other masters and companions of the above-mentioned profession, have updated and clarified the old traditions, and we have come together in a fraternal spirit in this assembly and have pledged to observe faithfully the regulations that are defined below. We make this pledge for ourselves and for our successors.*

1. Whoever wishes to join our fraternal organization must promise to respect all the points and articles that are mentioned in this book.

2. If a worker who had begun an honestly conceived work were to die, it is necessary that any other master who is an expert in his area be able to continue the work and lead it to a successful completion.

3. If a companion who is competent in the subject applies for and desires promotion, after having served in this area, he may be accepted.

4. If a master dies before completing the work he undertook and if another master takes it up, he must complete it and not give it up to a third person; this is so that those who commissioned the work in question are not involved in excessive expenses that would be harmful to the memory of the deceased.

5. If a new building site is opened where there was not one before, or if a master dies and is replaced by another one, who is not a member of this corporation, the master who holds the documents and the statutes of the corporation, and who has authority over this region, must choose a replacement master for this corporation and have him swear and promise to maintain everything in good order, according to the laws of the masons and stoneworkers. Whoever is opposed to this law may not receive any support from any companion or master, and no companion of this corporation may enter his building site.

6. Whoever depends on a lord, whether he be a master or a companion, may not be accepted into the corporation except with the agreement of his lord.

7. If a building site was set up, for example, in Strasbourg, Cologne, Vienna, Passau, or in other such places, nobody coming from the outside should profit from it.

8. The master who enters into such an enterprise (that is ongoing) must maintain the salary that was in effect until then.

9. The agreed-upon salary must go entirely to the companions who were involved in the work from the beginning.

10. He must, in all respects, behave correctly toward the companions, in accordance with the rights and customs of stonecutters and masons, and in accordance with the customs of the region.

11. If a master has undertaken work on a building site, and if other masters pass by, they should in no way accept a position there unless the first one has given up working on that project. Naturally, they must be competent.

12. The masters in question should do their work in such a way that the building built by them be without flaws for the length of time that is determined by the customs of their region.

13. If it suits a master to undertake another project concurrently with his own, and if he is unable to complete it successfully, and if another master takes it up, the latter should make sure that it is completed, so that the project does not remain unfinished. But if he does not have the competence needed to finish it properly, he should be questioned and punished, so that it may be ascertained what he has done wrong.

14. The master or masters who undertake such work may not hire the services of anyone, except those who are competent in this domain.

15. If a master takes up work for which he is not competent, no companion should assist him.

16. Two masters should not undertake to do the same work, unless the work can be finished in the course of the same year.

17. Any master who resides on his building site may not have more than two assistants. And if he were to have one or more external building sites, he cannot have more than two assistants on each of them, so that he does not have more than five assistants on all of his building sites. But if he loses a building site, he must employ the assistants from that one on his other building sites, until the period for which he hired them has expired, and he should not hire other assistants until that work is completed.

18. If a master is lacking one assistant,

he may hire another one, for such time until the first one's contract has expired.

**19.** When an assistant serves a master in accordance with the statutes of the corporation, and if the master has promised that he would give him some specific work projects and if the assistant wants to take advantage of those offers, he may rightfully come to an agreement with the master to work longer for him.

**20.** Any contractor who is directing a building site and to whom legal power over this corporation has been given, so that he may sort out any disputes that may arise among the builders, should be obeyed by all of the masters, companions, and assistants.

**21.** If a master receives a complaint, he should not pronounce a judgment by himself but must meet with the two closest other masters and the companions who belong to this building site. Together, they will shed light on the question, which will then be brought before the whole corporation.

**22.** Every master who has responsibility for the statutes of the corporation must have them read to his companions once a year, and if, in the course of the year, a master or companion asks to see the statutes, in whole or in part, he must inform him of what they are, so that there be no uncertainty.

**23.** If two or more masters belonging to this corporation have any dispute on subjects external to the profession, they should not seek help from outside the corporation, which will judge the matter as best it can.

**24.** No contractor or master may live openly with a woman to whom he is not married. If he does not refrain from doing so, no companion or stonecutter should remain on his building site or have anything to do with him.

**25.** In order that the spirit of brotherhood may remain whole and under divine protection, every master who is in charge of a building site must, as soon as he is received into the community, pay one gulden.

**26.** Each of the masters and contractors should have a chest, into which every companion must drop one pfennig each week. Every master must collect this money and any other sum that was put into the chest, and hand it over to the corporation every year.

**27.** Donations and fines should be paid into the chests of the community, in order that the divine service may be celebrated as well as possible.

**28.** If a contractor does not submit to the regulations and nonetheless wishes to exercise his profession, no companion may set foot on his building site, and the other masters should ignore him.

**29.** If a master has still not entered the corporation, if he does not declare himself hostile to the corporation and takes a companion, he will not be punished for that action.

**30.** If a companion goes to another master, who leads an honest life, asking to be hired, he may be employed for as long as he continues to fulfill his obligations with respect to the corporation.

**31.** And if it should happen that a complaint is made by a master against another master, by a companion against another companion, or against a master, these complaints should be brought before the masters who hold the books of the corporation.

**32.** One may not admit into the corporation any master or contractor who has not received Holy Communion in the previous year, or who does not practice the faith, or who wastes his money on gambling. If, by any chance, someone of that category has been co-opted, no master or companion should have any contact with him until he has changed his way of life and has been punished by the community.

◆ The building of Athens, from a fifteenth-century miniature.

**33.** The master who is in charge of the books must promise the corporation that he will look after them and that he will not let anybody copy them, and will not lend them to anyone, so that they may remain intact. But if anybody in the corporation needs to copy one or two articles, he may be loaned the books or permitted to copy them.

**34.** If a master or companion copies a book without the knowledge of the master who is the author of that book, he shall be expelled from the corporation; no master or companion shall have any contact with him and no companion shall have anything to do with his works until he has made honorable amends.

**35.** In addition, having undertaken a project of work and drawn up a plan, a master must not modify that plan but must carry it out in accordance with the customs of the country.

**36.** If a master or companion incurs expenses on behalf of the community, he must justify them and the community should reimburse him. If anybody has any problems with the Law, or in any other circumstances that concern the corporation, it owes him assistance and protection.

**37.** If a master or a companion is in difficulty with the law, or with anything else, everyone, whether he be a master or a companion, owes him assistance and help, in accordance with the commitments of the corporation.

**38.** If a master has not received the full payment due to him for the building, once it is finished, he is not authorized to charge interest. On the other hand, a master who has advanced money to a person or a city, in order to bring a building project to its successful completion, must also not charge interest.

**39.** If a master has to build foundations and is unable to complete the job because of the lack of a qualified workforce, he is completely free to hire masons, so that the people or the cities who commissioned the work are not left in a difficult situation.

**40.** All the masters and companions who have undertaken, under oath, to respect the regulations of the corporation, must be faithful to their pledges. If a master or companion infringes any of the articles of the regulations, he must atone for this and will be bound to respect the relevant article.

**41.** In Ratisbon, it has been decided that: Master Jost Dotzinger, who built our cathedral and several other religious establishments in Strasbourg, will be considered the president and judge, and this will also apply to his successors and to Speyer as well as to Strasbourg.

**42.** All the masters who own a chest on the building sites where there is no chest belonging to the corporation shall be accountable for the finances to the masters who hold the books of the corporation, and a religious service shall be celebrated in the place where the books are kept. In the event of the death of a master or of a companion, on a building site where there is no corporation book, this death will be announced to the master who holds the books of the corporation. As soon as the announcement of the death reaches him, he must have a mass said for the repose of the soul of the deceased. All the masters and companions should be present and should make a small financial contribution.

**43.** On a building site where a corporate book is kept, the contents of the chests of the nearest building sites should be collected together.

**44.** No master or companion who does not belong to the corporation may receive the slightest training.

**45.** One does not have the right to receive money as payment for the teaching one gives, but nothing prevents a master from teaching without pay all those who wish to study with him.

**46.** If a pious person wishes to take part in the religious services, he should be welcomed, provided that he pays an initial fee, followed by annual dues. But, apart from the divine services, he must not participate in the work of the corporation.

**47.** In the year 1459, four weeks before Easter, the masters and the workers of this corporation, who have come to Ratisbon, have sworn loyalty on the book.

—Jost Dotzinger,
the master of the works
of Strasbourg Cathedral

✦ *Pages 172–73:* The cathedral
of Notre-Dame, Reims.

## REGULATIONS CONCERNING THE COMPANIONS

*(Extracts)*

**1.** If one or more companions, in the course of their Tour of Germany, come to work on these building sites, the master must ensure that they get the same salary that they received before. And if they have not previously sworn the oath, the master must have them carry out this formality. If they refuse, no one must hire them.

**2.** The master must not hire any companion who is leading a dissolute life or who is living with a concubine, or who does not go to confession once a year, and does not receive Holy Communion, or who wastes his salary by gambling.

**3.** If a companion comes to the workshop committee and asks to be hired, his request may not be granted unless the person with whom he served his apprenticeship was himself a master mason.

**4.** The candidate should not speak to anyone else, at the risk of being punished.

**5.** Every traveling companion who is employed on a project must obey the master or his deputy, in accordance with the rules and customs of the corporation.

**6.** Every traveling companion who is employed on a construction project must not speak ill of his employer or insult his honor. But if the employer has infringed the rules of the corporation, anyone may denounce him.

**7.** When a journeyman leaves the project, he should not leave any debts or cause for complaints.

**8.** If an employer wishes to release a journeyman, he should only discharge him on a Saturday or on the evening of a payday, so that he will be able to travel the next day, unless there is a valid reason why he should act differently.

**9.** A speaker (supervisor or cement mixer) should serve his master faithfully, in accordance with the law and with custom; he should never do him any harm, by action or words, either in person or via intermediaries.

**10.** Every traveling companion should promise the members of the corporation that he will respect all the corporate rules and whoever refuses to do this, or who commits an offense, should not be hired by any contractor who may hear about it.

**11.** If a master or a companion of the corporation falls ill, and if he cannot provide for his own needs, the corporation owes him assistance and support and, if he is in need, it should lend him the money necessary for his care, which he will commit himself to paying back later. If he should die, whatever he has left behind (clothes or other possessions) should be seized until the costs have been recovered.

**12.** If a companion arrives at the office of a master who does not have the book of the corporation and asks for employment, the master may hire him, first signing him up as a member of the corporation and giving him the regulation salary. If the master has no more money, he shall recommend the companion to the nearest of his colleagues who holds the corporation's book and chests. The statutes should be read to the companion and he must swear to respect them.

**13.** If a companion has served a mason and not a contractor, and if he wants to join the corporation, he must work for a contractor without a salary for two years. If he does not accept this, he will not be admitted into the corporation. In any case, every master who holds a corporation book must act according to the circumstances.

## REGULATIONS CONCERNING THE APPRENTICES

**1.** No master or contractor may hire an apprentice who is not married. In addition, it is right to ask him whether his mother and father are married.

**2.** No master or contractor may hire an assistant for a length of time that is shorter than six years.

**3.** Nor should he make him a foreman before this length of time has expired.

**4.** Nor should he make him a foreman until he has completed a tour lasting one year, as a journeyman.

**5.** The master or the contractor must have the apprentice promise to respect the terms of the rules of the corporation.

**6.** If an apprentice leaves his employer without a legitimate reason, before the period for which he was to serve has expired, no other employer may hire him. No companion may associate with him before he returns to his employer, with whom he must complete the length of his apprenticeship and give him every satisfaction, in acknowledgment of which he will receive a certificate. No apprentice may pay his employer any compensation, except in the case of marriage, when the employer agrees to it, or for any other legitimate reason that compels him or his employer to do so.

**7.** If an apprentice has the impression that his master has done him some harm, he may bring the matter before the contractor and the masters of the region, at the risk, however, of being ousted and of having to go elsewhere.

**8.** If an apprentice behaves badly, from the point of view of his personal life and in his relations with a woman outside marriage, he shall lose the profits of his years of apprenticeship; his case must nevertheless be examined with understanding.

**9.** If a master, companion, or apprentice has infringed the rules, he must obediently accept his punishment. If one of them refuses to do so, he must be excluded from the corporation until he has been punished. He should be avoided and despised by all.

*Decrees and Articles of
the Guild of Stonecutters of the
Grand Lodge of Strasbourg*

## THE STATUTES
## OF SAINT MICHAEL
## (1563)

### First article of the decrees:

**1.** In case some of the articles of this book prove to be too severe or punitive, or others too liberal, those who are members of our guild may, by a majority vote, modify, censor, or amend the said articles, in accordance with the time period, the requirements of the country concerned, and the course of developments. And when there is a general meeting, the members shall gather together in the form of a chapter, in accordance with the rules set out in this book; their decisions must be consistent with the oath that everybody has sworn.

### On the duties of the members of the guild:

**2.** Whoever enters this guild by his own free will must promise, as a member of our corporation of masons, to uphold each of these points and articles, as they appear in this book. The masters will be those members who are able to put up magnificent buildings and other similar projects, for which they have received authorization, and who do not serve any corporation other than the one that they have chosen to serve. Masters or companions have the obligation to behave honorably and must not cause anyone any harm. As a consequence, we have made provisions in these statutes to

punish them in case any such acts were to take place.

### On the authorization to perform work by the day:

**3.** As certain regular tasks are considered and paid for by the day, whether in Strasbourg, Cologne, Vienna, or on other, similar building sites, by the lodges attached to them, and in view of this established custom, the construction and other work associated with this practice will continue to be treated as daily work; and in no case will a contract be drawn up, in order that the work not be interrupted, in as much as that is possible, because of the existence of such a contract.

### Who may apply for work:

**4.** If a craftsman who has been given a regular work assignment were to die, any craftsman or master who is skilled in masonry and who is qualified enough to do the job may apply for it and may present himself to those of the masters who are in charge of the project, in order that they may proceed to find a replacement worker, according to the requirements of the construction project. This is true of any companion who is skilled in masonry.

### The work has to be allocated daily:

**5.** Although it may suit a master, in addition to his own work, to accept an outside assignment of work, he cannot be authorized to do this unless he has entrusted another qualified master with the responsibility for that work; he must vouch for the fact that the work will continue according to plan and that there is no risk of it being interrupted, and such building or construction work will be paid for on a daily basis. According to the rights and customs of masonry, if a master does not respect this rule in the case of persons who have worked on the proj-

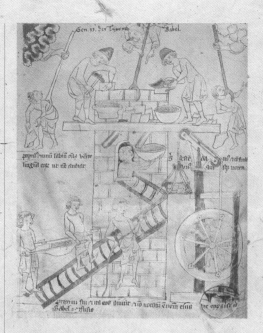

♦ The Tower of Babel, from a fourteenth-century miniature.

ect from the beginning, and if this is discovered in the course of a reputable investigation, the said master must be reprimanded by the order, and expelled, and punished, if the case against him has been proved. But, if the project directors do not agree to this, they shall have the power to decide what to do.

### The death of a master during a building project:

**6.** In the case of the death of a master who is in charge of a building project, or who was involved in it and where the stones he has cut are found by another master, who applies for the job, whether those stones have been laid or not, the new master must not assemble the work to be done with the cut stones, or in any case abandon the stonework that has not been laid, without the consent and agreement of the other members of the corporation, so that the masters of the works and other honorable persons who were involved in planning the project are not obliged to incur unjustified expenses, and that the master who left such a project does not have his good name defamed after his death. But if the masters of the works wish such work to be canceled or withdrawn, then the new master may accomplish it, on condition that he does not seek to draw any dishonest gain from it.

### How to manage the stonecutting and building work:

**7.** Authorization will be given to any master who has practiced the building trade with a mason and stonecutter for five years; he will have the power to cut stone and to build according to a contract or by the workday, and he will be able to do so without fear, if he so wishes, but he must not infringe the articles stated above or below.

### When a master presents a plan for a building project:

**8.** If someone signs a contract for a project and presents a plan for the way in which it is to be executed, the work may not in any way be modified, in relation to the original design. He must execute it strictly according to the plan that was shown to the patron, whether he be a lord, a city, or an individual, so that nothing is missing from the building. If, however, the client wishes that a change be made, only then can it be carried out, but the worker must not seek any undue profit or advantage arising from any change.

### What kind of work can two masters work on jointly?

**9.** Two masters cannot work jointly on a construction or building project, unless it is a small project that may be completed in the space of one year; if that is the case, a master may work with a companion from the city.

### On the work required of masons:

**10.** A master may permit masons to be employed in accordance with the following principles:

- If masons are needed for the foundations or to build a wall for which they are qualified, the master may employ them in order that the patron does not experience any delay in the completion of the project.
- Those who are employed but are not subject to these regulations will not be asked to cut and sculpt columns, because they have not served for the time stated in our regulations.

### A person who drives another off a project:

**11.** Whoever he may be, whether a master or a companion, any person who drives another master, who is a member of the guild, to leave his work (be it major or minor), or who tries to do so, openly or secretly and without the other person's knowledge or consent, shall be taken to task; and no master or companion shall have anything to do with him, and no companion of the guild shall enter his service for as long as he controls the work that he obtained in a dishonorable way, or until he has made restitution and made whole the person he deprived of the job; and until he has been punished by the masters who are charged with this task in the name of the guild.

### Who may accept a job in sculpted or cut stone:

**12.** If a person wishes to take up a job in sculpted or cut stone and does not know how to execute it according to the original working drawings, without having served his time in the corporation, or having been employed in a lodge, then he should not reasonably undertake such a job. But if he does undertake it, in that case no companion may remain at his side or work for him, in order that the master of the works shall not be made to incur inappropriate expenses through the fault of such a foolish master.

### Who may learn to execute a project according to the basic working drawings or any other work of sculpture?

**13.** No master, supervisor, or companion shall teach anyone who is not a member of the corporation to copy extracts from the basic working drawings, or other aspects of masonry, or anyone else who has not already practiced masonry, or who has served for a long enough time with a mason, according to our trade, customs, and regulations.

### No master shall teach a companion in exchange for money:

**14.** No craftsman or master shall ask a companion for money to show or teach him anything related to masonry. In the same way, no supervisor or companion shall teach or instruct anyone in sculpture in exchange for payment, as stated above. However, if a person wishes to instruct or teach another, he can do so by executing part of the other person's work, either out of friendship for the companion, or as a service to their master.

### How many apprentices may a master have?

**15.** A master who has only one building project may have three apprentices, two who roughly shape the stones, and one who finishes them off; this is so that he may also employ some companions from the same lodge, if his superiors authorize him to do so. If he has more than one building, he shall not have more than two apprentices on the first project or building, in such a way that he does not have more than five apprentices throughout all of his building sites. These measures are taken in order that they may serve their five years on the construction project on which he is working.

### A person who is living openly with a concubine:

**16.** No craftsman or master shall live openly with a concubine. If, however, such a person does not wish to stop living in this state, no traveling companion or stonecutter shall remain in his service or have any relations with him.

### A person who is not living as a Christian and who does not receive Holy Communion once a year:

**17.** No craftsman or master shall be admitted into the guild if he does not receive the Holy Sacrament once a year, or does not respect Christian discipline, or if he wastes his wages by gambling. But if anyone who was inadvertently admitted into the guild does not respect the above-mentioned principles, no master shall have any relations with him, and no companion shall remain with him, until such a time as he stops doing this and is punished by the members of the guild.

### If a companion works for a master who has not been promoted within this guild:

**18.** If a companion accepts work from a master who has not been promoted in this craftsmen's guild, he shall not be liable to be punished. In the same way, if a companion applies to a master in the city, and obtains a job, he is authorized to do so in order that every companion may find work. But the companion must respect the written rules, as stated above and below. It is right that he should give the guild what he should give, even though he is not in one of the lodges of the guild, or united with his brother companions. If a companion wishes legitimately to get married, and not to be employed in a lodge, or does so in order to set up in business in a city, he must pay four centimes every quarter, for as long as he is no longer employed in a lodge.

### How complaints are to be heard and judged and sanctions imposed:

**19.** If a master makes a complaint against another master, for having violated the regulations of the corporation, or similarly, a master makes one against a companion, or a companion against another companion, or in any other case in which a master and a companion are involved, the master who holds the book of regulations shall be informed of it. And the master who receives such information must listen to both parties and set a date

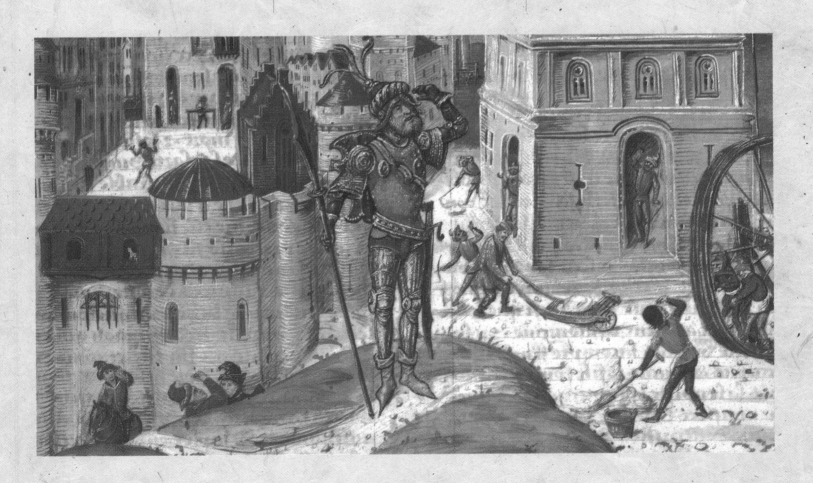

♦ The building of the Tower of Babel, from a fifteenth-century manuscript.

when he will hear their case. And during the period that precedes the day set aside for that hearing, no companion may avoid the master or a master a companion, but they should help each other out mutually until the hour at which the dispute is heard and resolved. All this will be done in accordance with the judgment of the corporation and all decisions will therefore be respected. Moreover, the dispute will be decided where it arose, by the master holding the book of regulations for the district involved, and who lives closest to where the dispute has arisen.

### Concerning expulsion:

**20.** In addition, concerning expulsion, it has been decided that: if an allegation is brought against a master or a companion, of something that was learned by hearsay and repeated from one person to another, for as long as the facts of the matter in question have not been established, according to the procedures, the accused person shall be neither avoided nor expelled by anybody and shall continue to do his work until the decision has been sent to him at his home, and only after it has been established in accordance with the regulations. Until this has been done, he shall continue to obey the laws of the corporation and nobody shall have the power to take action against him according to our regulations.

### No appeals are to be made:

**21.** It is also resolved that a case shall be judged wherever it arose and developed, or if that is not possible, in the nearest lodge that is in possession of the book. And no party shall appeal until the complaint and response have been heard. The complaint cannot be taken further unless it is rejected at that level.

### Complaints that the master has the authority to hear:

**22.** Every master of the works who has work in his lodge and who has been given the text of these statutes and the authority to enforce them has the power and the authority to hear and decide on a punishment in all cases of faults and disputes that are connected with masonry. All of the masters, supervisors, and companions owe him obedience.

### Every master shall behave in accordance with the regulations and shall take them as a guide:

**23.** On this day in Strasbourg, in the year 1563, it has been decided that every master who is entrusted with a long-term construction project, and not with a short-term one, whether in principalities, countries, cities, leagues, or cloisters, shall sit in judgment in accordance with our regulations. A considerable increase in benefits will result from this and much harm will be avoided for those who have to do building work. Consequently, each of them shall have a book and will be recognized as the superior officer of his jurisdiction or district, by all of the masters and companions of this province. He will also have the delegation of power deriving from each of the members of this assembly, in order that he may, jointly with his masters and companions, in view of their superior status, lead this corporation, punish its subjects, admit brothers, assist the sick, and organize a general assembly of the members from the region, while respecting the regulations in all that he does.

### Where the book is is where the chest for the poor and the sick should be:

**24.** All those to whom the book has been entrusted should faithfully collect the weekly centimes of the companions; if a companion falls ill, they should assist him. Where a master has other masters and companions under his authority, he has the responsibility of collecting the weekly centime in a chest. The chest reserved for this purpose shall be emptied and the contents counted in front of each district superior every year and its contents shall be used to help the poor and the sick of our corporation who come under his jurisdiction. Each master who is entrusted with a chest and who has annually received the total amount in the chests of his neighbors shall send, every year, on Saint Michael's Day, one "Bohemian" to the primary lodge in Strasbourg, with a note stating where it comes from, as a sign of obedience and of brotherly love, and in order that it be known that all the things stated above have been accomplished.

### The locations where the books are kept depend on the Grand Lodge of Strasbourg:

**25.** Speyer, Zürich, Augsburg, Frankfurt, Ulm, Heilbronn, Blassenburg, Dresden, Nuremberg, Salzburg, Mentz, Stuttgart, Heidelberg, Freiburg, Basel, Haguenau, Schlestadt, Regensburg, Meyenheim, Munich, Anspach, and Constance.

### Concerning any companion who wishes to serve a master for a time:

**26.** If the companion has traveled and served the corporation and is already a member of the guild and wishes to serve a craftsman for a time, the said master and the worker will not accept one or the other for less than one year, or approximately that length of time.

### Concerning a master or companion who does not apply these regulations:

**27.** All of those who are members of the

guild, masters or companions, must respect all the points and articles, as they are written down above and below. But if by some chance a person does not respect these points, he may be punished; if he agrees to obey the rules and pays the fine that has been imposed on him, this will be sufficient for him to be considered absolved of any obligation relating to the article for which he was penalized.

### How the masters of the guild must look after the book:

**28.** The master who is in charge of the book must swear an oath before the guild and promise that it will not be copied by him or by any other person, and that it will not be loaned to anyone. This is so that the books may retain their full power, as the corporation has decided. But if anyone needs to see one or two articles, the master can give them to him in writing. Every master must also arrange to have these regulations read out, every year, in front of the companions, assembled in the lodge.

### Concerning the penalties that may lead to expulsion from the corporation:

**29.** If a complaint that is liable to involve a more serious punishment is presented before the master or if, for example, somebody is to be forbidden from entering the corporation, the master may not hear or judge the case alone. He must, instead, ask for the assistance of the two masters who live closest to him, who are in possession of the book and have been given authority in accordance with the regulations, in such a way that there are three of them, and he must also call on the companions who are employed where the complaint was presented, in order that the three masters may decide, under oath and to the best of their judgment, what the whole corporation is to do about the matter.

### When quarrels not concerning masonry arise:

**30.** If two or more masters who are members of the guild have diverging opinions or are in dispute about a subject that does not concern masonry, they should not summon a member to appear, because of that dispute, anywhere other than before the corporation and brotherhood, where they will be judged and reconciled, to the best of their ability and in such a way that the matter may be resolved without prejudice to the rights of the patron (lords or cities), in the place where the case first arose.

### What each master or companion must contribute to, in respect of the guild:

**31.** Now, in order that the regulations be respected as honestly as possible, in the service of God, for other needs and all similar matters, each master who is employed in the lodge and who practices masonry and belongs to this guild must, at the time of his admission, first pay one florin, and in every subsequent year pay two "Bohemians" or "blapperts" into the chest, or five "Bohemians" if he is a companion, and an apprentice must pay the same amount once he has served his time.

### What are the chests that the masters must have and what should they distribute from their contents?

**32.** All the masters and other members of this guild who are employed in the lodge must possess a chest and every companion has to pay one centime a week into it. Every master must faithfully collect this money and all that may also be due. The contents of the chest must be taken every year to the guild accounting office, in the place where the nearest book is kept, so that relief may be

+ King Edward I's masons hard at work.

+ *Pages 180–81:* Gallery of the cathedral of Laon.

given to the poor and that the needs of the guild may be taken care of.

### When a master does not fulfill his duty in respect of an apprentice companion in the trade:

**33.** If an apprentice considers that a master is not fulfilling his duty toward him in any respect, as he agreed to do, the apprentice may bring the matter before the corporation and the masters who reside in that area, for a full investigation and in order that he may continue his journey, according to the circumstances.

### What should be done in this fraternal association if someone is sick:

**34.** If a master or a companion falls ill or if a member of the guild who has spent his time as a law-abiding mason falls ill, and therefore cannot ensure his livelihood or obtain the necessities of life, the master who has the chest and who is responsible for it must help him and assist him with a loan from the chest, if nothing else can be done and until such a time as he has recovered his health. The said member will have to promise to return the money borrowed from the chest; but if he should die, in the course of that illness, a portion of his clothing or other belongings equivalent to the sum he was loaned will be confiscated, if that proves possible, out of the total assets left after his death.

### If someone incurs expenses on behalf of the fraternal guild:

**35.** If a master or a mason incurs expenses or pays any costs on behalf of the guild, he must provide a justification and explain the reasons for those large or small expenses, which will then be paid back to the master or companion by a withdrawal from the chest of the guild. Similarly, if someone is having problems with the law or with others concerning

✦ Gaïa, from a fifteenth-century miniature.

the guild, then everyone, whether a master or a companion, must be helpful to him and must give him assistance, in keeping with the oath of the guild. However, no one may involve the fraternal guild in any expenses on his own initiative, without seeking the advice of the other masters and companions.

### How someone who disobeys should be punished:

**36.** If masters, supervisors, or apprentices were in any way to disobey the articles or the points that follow, and were not to respect them, either collectively or individually, and if this were to be discovered by an honorable procedure, they would be summoned to appear before the corporation, to be asked about those actions. And they would be given punishments and penalties in accordance with the oath and the commitments that everybody took in respect of the guild. But if anyone scorns the punishment or the

summons without a valid reason, and does not appear, the punishment will nonetheless be imposed for his disobedience, even if he is not present. If he does not respect it, he will not be permitted to do anything at all and no stonecutter must remain with him until he obeys the authorities again.

### Who will be the superior judge in this corporation?

**37.** Marx Schan, master of the works of the high institution of our dear Mother in Strasbourg, and all his successors.

### The following area comes under the authority of Strasbourg:

**38.** All of the region north of the Moselle and Franconia up to the forest of Thuringia, and Babenberg up to the bishopric of Eichstatten, and from Eichstatten to Ulm, from Ulm to Augsburg, and from Augsburg to Adelberg and as far as Italy, and the regions of Meissen, Hesse, and Swabia, must all respect these regulations.

### The following district belongs to Vienna:

**39.** To the master of the works of Saint Stephen in Vienna belong: Lampach, Styria, Werkhausen, Hungary, and the lower valley of the Danube.

### The following area belongs to Cologne:

**40.** To the master of the works of the foundation of Cologne and to all his successors belong the territories that remain in the south, and they must be obeyed in the same way, whether they are projects or lodges that are already members of the guild, or that might become members later.

### The following district belongs to Zürich:

**41.** Bern, Basel, Lucerne, Schaffhausen,

Saint-Gallen, etc., and all the current projects that are in the Swiss Confederation or that may join it later, owe obedience to the Master of Zürich.

### Regulations of the supervisors and companions of the Corporation of Stonemasons:

**42.** Every supervisor must honor his master, must be diligent and respectful toward him, in accordance with the rule of masonry, and must obey him with total faithfulness, as this has been practiced in ancient customs. And a companion must do the same.

### If someone wishes to travel, he must ask for permission to leave:

**43.** If it pleases a companion to pursue his travels, he must take leave of his master, of his lodge, and of his hostelry in such a way as not to owe anyone anything, and not to give anyone any reason to reproach him for it at a later meeting.

### How the companions must obey the masters and the supervisors:

**44.** A companion entering any lodge in which he is employed must obey its master and its supervisors, in accordance with the rule and the ancient customs of masonry, and must also respect all the rules and privileges that have long been in effect in the said lodge.

### No companion will disrupt his master's work:

**45.** A companion must not criticize the work of his master either secretly or openly, or in any way, except if the master infringes the rules or acts contrary to the regulations and everyone knows about it and can testify to it.

### No companion living in a state of adultery may be given employment:

**46.** No master or craftsman shall employ a companion who is living in a state of adultery with a woman, or who is living a dishonorable life with women, or who does not go to Holy Communion in accordance with Christian teaching, or who is foolish enough to gamble away his clothes.

### If a companion arbitrarily decides to quit:

**47.** If a companion were arbitrarily to decide to leave a main lodge or any other lodge, the master and the companions of the said lodge should not allow him to leave without being penalized.

### No one is to be released except at the end of a payday:

**48.** If a craftsman or master of the works wishes to release a companion who is working for him, he must not dismiss him on any day other than a Saturday or on the evening of a payday, so that he may be in a position to know how to travel the next day, and unless he has given cause for offense. The same principle should also be respected by a companion who asks to be released.

### To obtain a job, one should ask no one except the master or the supervisor:

**49.** And to obtain a job, no companion must ask anyone except the master or the supervisor of the lodge, either secretly or openly, or without their consent.

### There must be no conspiracies:

**50.** Similarly, the companions must not mutiny or conspire to leave a job collectively, thereby delaying the building work, because until now the benefits of our brotherhood have been derived, almost exclusively, from the lords and the cities. But if a master behaves improperly in any case that may arise, he will be summoned to appear before the corporation and judged. During the period of the trial, such a master must not be avoided by his companions until the judgment has been announced, unless he does not respect the judgment, in which case he may be ignored.

### One must not leave the lodge without permission:

**51.** No companion should leave the lodge without permission or, if he is going out for bread or other meals, he must not remain outside without getting authorization to do so. No one shall abstain from working on Monday. If anyone were to do so, he should be punished by the master and the companions, and the master would have the power to dismiss him at any time of the week.

### No beatings:

**52.** And, in the future, no one shall be beaten in any lodge or for any reason, without the master's prior knowledge and consent. And nothing is to be judged and tried by the master or the companions, on the building site or elsewhere, without the knowledge of the chief master of the works, or his consent to the trial and punishment.

### No talking in the lodge:

**53.** And in the future, the companions must wait in the lodge before their prayer, and must not continue chatting, in order that the masters not be disturbed in their work.

### What an apprentice must promise the corporation when he has served his time and is declared free:

**54.** First, every apprentice who has served his time and who is declared free must promise the corporation, by giving his word of honor, under oath and under penalty of losing his right to practice masonry, that he will not communicate or reveal to anyone the masonic greeting and handshake, except to a person to whom he may do so according to the rules, and also that he will not write anything down about it. Second, he must promise, as is stated above, to obey the masonic corporation in all matters having to do with the corporation, and if he were to be judged by the corporation, that he would entirely submit to the judgment and would accept it. Third, he must promise not to weaken but, on the contrary, to strengthen the corporation in so far as he is able to do so. Fourth, no one must cut stones next to anyone who is not a regular member of the corporation, and no master may employ for the cutting of stone anyone who is not a true stonecutter, unless he has first obtained the permission of the whole corporation.

**55.** And no one must, by his own will and authority, change the mason's mark that the corporation has given him. If he wishes to change it, he may only do so with the good will and approval of the corporation, which must have been informed of it.

**56.** And every master who has such apprentices must loyally encourage and invite each one who has completed the aforementioned five-year term to become a brother, by virtue of the individual oath that he has pronounced before the corporation.

## No apprentice can be a student supervisor:

**57.** No craftsman or master may designate as supervisor any one of the apprentices he has accepted and, who are still serving the years of their apprenticeship.

**58.** And no craftsman or master may designate as supervisor an apprentice whom he accepted when he was starting out, even if he has served his time of apprenticeship, unless he has traveled for a year.

## Regulations concerning the apprentices:

**59.** A person who accepts an apprentice must not do so without charging a security payment of any less than twenty florins, which he must deposit with someone who lives in the same place, so that if the master should die before the end of the apprenticeship, the apprentice may serve the corporation with another true master and may complete the entire five years. But if he does not complete this period, he will give up the twenty florins to the corporation, to cover his expenses and losses, in the same way that he would owe the master a sum of money, because he was leaving him without a valid reason during his apprenticeship. The purpose of this is to encourage the apprentices to persevere and to become true stonecutters.

**60.** And no member of the corporation must knowingly accept an apprentice of illegitimate birth. Reasonable inquiries must be made before he is accepted and the apprentice must be asked, on his word of honor, whether his father and mother have lived together in the bonds of marriage.

**61.** It has also been decided that no craftsman may take on an apprentice for less than five years, and consequently, no person may pay money for the time that he has not served but must serve his five years in full. From now on, no other arrangements are possible, whatever may have been done in the past or is currently being done.

**62.** A father who is himself a mason is authorized to take on one or more of his own sons for five years and to complete their training; but he may do so only in the presence of other stonecutters. Such an apprentice may not be less than fourteen years old.

**63.** If a person has served a mason who is not a stonecutter for a certain period of time, that time must not be counted in or deducted from the five years of apprenticeship; but he must work for a stonecutter for five years, as was stated above.

**64.** Consequently, no master shall accept an apprentice who is starting out or shall declare him free, except in the presence of the corporation and the companions who are at the time employed in the lodge, so that any disagreements or mistakes, if they should arise, may easily be resolved.

**65.** And every apprentice must promise the corporation, on his word of honor, to obey his master for the five years during which he is tied to him, and to serve him loyally, genuinely, and faithfully, to his greatest benefit and to spare him any loss, insofar as that is in his power, and without any exception or restriction.

**66.** And the master, for his part, must for the said five years, according to the ancient ways and customs of the corporation, give his apprentice ten florins, that is two florins per year, as a salary, in addition to his food and keep.

**67.** He must promise to be loyal and obedient to the corporation, worthy in all things concerning the corporation, and if a dispute or disagreement were to arise with the master or with another stonecutter or the apprentices, he must present the matter in question before the corporation for a hearing and resolution, in order that he may obtain justice and a judgment in all things, good and bad, according to the rules of the corporation, and he must not appeal against the verdict that is announced but accept it entirely.

**68.** In addition, nothing shall be kept secret from someone who has been accepted and declared free; but everything that should be said or read to him will be transmitted to him, so that nobody can complain or use the excuse that if he had known this earlier, he would not have joined the corporation.

**69.** And in every case, a card must be prepared, which is divided into two parts by a cut of a specific pattern, one of which will be kept in the lodge, and the other with the security payment, in such a way that each party may know what to do.

**70.** And every master who takes on an apprentice must pay the sum of five "Bohemians" or "blappers," but not more, to the corporation. Similarly, when the apprentice is declared free, he will be asked to pay one florin, but never more, to be spent on drinks for those who are present and who witness the granting of that freedom.

**71.** And no master must prolong by more than fourteen days the trial period of a beginning apprentice, whose age is that stipulated by the articles, unless he is his own son, or unless the master has a valid reason for this delay, having to do with the security payment, for example, and not with an evil purpose in mind.

### When someone leaves during his apprenticeship:

**72.** If it should happen that an apprentice were to leave his master during his years of apprenticeship, without a valid reason, and thus did not serve his full term, no master must employ such an apprentice and no one must remain near him or have any company with him, un-

til he has served his years in an honorable way, with the master whom he left, and until he has made honorable amends and brought written confirmation that he has done so from his master. And no apprentice may ask for a refund of the security payment, unless he is getting married, with his master's consent, or unless he has other valid reasons, which compel him or his master to make this request, and this may only be granted if the brotherhood has been informed and following a judgment made by the stonecutters.

♦ This detail from a fifteenth-century engraving depicts Noah having his ark built.

### Apprentices must not be incited to leave:

**73.** No master or companion, whatever his title may be, may incite an apprentice who is tied to him to leave, or dismiss him, or take on another one, who has come from somewhere else, unless he has first obtained the authorization of his master, in such a way that he may leave him without any grievance. But if this were to happen, the master responsible must be brought before the corporation and punished.

# Conclusion

As we stand on the brink of the twenty-first century, more and more people are visiting cathedrals. Chance visits or carefully planned ones, visits of discovery or for a prayer, trips as part of a pilgrimage, one-time or repeat visits—people's reasons or motives for stopping in are many and varied. It is happening throughout Europe, wherever there are cathedrals, from Prague to Paris, from Freiburg to Cologne and Lausanne.

For each of these people, the atmosphere and tranquility of the cathedral present a strong contrast with the outside world. Modern life and its noises seem foreign to a building that is regarded not as anachronistic but rather as timeless. In this way, just as it did centuries ago, the cathedral fulfills a dual function, one that is both material and symbolic: it is material as a building, and symbolic through its ability to mediate between the visible and the invisible world.

The message of the people who built the cathedrals is, nevertheless, rarely apprehended in its entirety since very few visitors take the time truly to "read" and understand the monument. But reading the cathedral presupposes, above all, that one has a knowledge of a technical, historical, and religious language that cannot be improvised. The readings that do take place are, therefore, often too hasty and incomplete. In fact, ever since the first cathedrals were built, they have offered us several levels at which they may be understood and appreciated, and no single meaning was codified and remains valid for ever. Everyone may thus legitimately understand the cathedral in relation to his or her own intellectual and spiritual journey, in accordance with the motives that caused one to enter a building that is so different from all others and from the city in which it stands.

A technical wonder? A moving symbol of transcendent faith? A place of history? A place of memory? Of prayer? Of renewal? The cathedral is all of those things and more, because beyond the Christian people for whom it was built, it calls out to the whole of humankind.

The cathedral sums up the final stage of human destiny: our appearance before the eternal truths. As an earthly monument, the cathedral speaks to humanity through symbols that majestically adorn its architecture. It reflects the skills of generations of human beings who collaborated to build it, but above all it stands as a vast witness to and illustration of an order that God imposed on the universe. In the cathedral, humans are at once small and great.

A complex and mysterious monument, the cathedral invites reflection on the meaning of life and stimulates a reconsideration of our place and of the meaning of our actions in society. This message was already well known to the people who built these masterpieces of architecture.

✦ *Opposite:* Claude Monet, *Rouen Cathedral.* 1894.

✦ *Page 188:* Labyrinth at Chartres Cathedral.

# List of Illustrations

**Page 50.** Seal of the workshops of the Cathedral of Notre-Dame, Strasbourg, Archives Municipales.

**Page 51.** Aisle of the Abbey Church of Pontigny (1130s–c. 1630); the aisles date from the 1150s. Pontigny, a Cistercian abbey, is in the early Gothic style, with groined vaults and arches, but without the flying buttresses that later made extreme height and walls of glass possible.

**Page 52.** Jean Fouquet (c. 1415–before 1481), *The Building of the Temple of Jerusalem, under the Order of Solomon,* miniature in an edition of Flavius Josephus, *Les Antiquités judaïques* (*The Jewish Wars*), c. 1465, Paris, Bibliothèque Nationale de France (MS. fr. 247, fol. 163). Fouquet represents the Temple of Jerusalem as the Cathedral of Tours, his hometown, thus deliberately conflating Old Testament history with more recent French history in a mixture of pious and propagandistic symbolism. The Gothic cathedral was begun in the 13th century, constructed for more than three hundred years, and destroyed in the 18th and 19th centuries, so Fouquet probably observed work done on it in his own lifetime, and his painting remains an important record of the building's probable form.

**Page 53.** The architect (or possibly Charlemagne) during the construction of the Cathedral of Aachen, detail of a medieval miniature from one of the French *Chroniques* (*Chronicles*) in Guillaume Crettin, *Recueil sommaire des croniques françoys* (*Collected French Chronicles*), compiled in the 17th century, Paris, Bibliothèque Nationale de France.

**Page 54.** Wooden model of the late Gothic pilgrimage church of Schöne Maria, based upon a design by the architect Hans Hieber (c. 1480–1521), c. 1520, Regensburg (Ratisbon), Museum der Stadt Regensburg. The church was begun by Hieber, and completed after his death.

**Page 55.** *An Architect Displays His Plans to a Lady*, 16th-century stained-glass window, Saint-Julien du Sault, Church of Saint-Pierre.

**Page 56.** Left: C. Studer, *Erwin von Steinbach Begins the Building of the Tower,* detail of a lithograph, 1840, Strasbourg, Bibliothèque Nationale et Universitaire (MS. CA 009). Right: A pair of architect's dividers, Troyes, Maison de l'Outil et de la Pensée Ouvrière.

**Page 57.** Detail of a manuscript illumination showing architect, king, and construction worker, in Matthew Paris (c. 1200–59), *The Book of Saint Albans*, c. 1245–52, Dublin, Trinity College Library (MS. 177, fol. 59v).

**Page 58.** Contract to hire the German architect Hans Hammer (d. 1519), master of works of Strasbourg Cathedral in 1486–90 and again in 1513–19, Strasbourg, Archives Municipales. Hammer continued the work of the previous architects, Ulrich von Ensingen (1360s–1419) and Johann Hültz (c. 1390–1449) on the cathedral, adding a late-Gothic touch.

**Page 59.** Detail of a drawing of the facade of the cathedral, Strasbourg, Musée de l'Oeuvre Notre-Dame.

**Pages 60–61.** Théophile Schuler, *The Building of Strasbourg Cathedral*, ink and watercolor, 1845, Strasbourg, Musée Historique.

**Pages 62–63.** Stonecutters and sculptors at work, stained-glass *Window of Saint Chéron,* 1220–30, Chartres, Cathedral of Notre-Dame.

**Page 63.** *The Grand Master of the Order of Knights Hospitaler of Rhodes Receives Masons and Carpenters,* detail of a miniature in Guillaume Caoursin, *De Bello Rhodio* (*On the War in Rhodes*), 15th century, Paris, Bibliothèque Nationale de France (MS. lat. 6067, fol. 9v).

**Page 64.** The architect (or possibly Charlemagne) during the construction of the Cathedral of Aachen, detail of a medieval miniature from one of the French *Chroniques* (*Chronicles*) in Guillaume Crettin, *Recueil sommaire des croniques françoys* (*Collected French Chronicles*), compiled in the 17th century, Paris, Bibliothèque Nationale de France.

**Page 65.** Tombstone of Hugues Libergier, architect, Reims, Cathedral of Notre-Dame.

**Page 66.** Detail of *How Alexander Had the Fort Constructed in Front of the Town,* miniature attributed to Willem Vrelant, in Jean Wauquelin, *Grand Alexandre* (*Romance of Alexander*), commissioned by Philip the Good, mid-15th century, Paris, Petit Palais (fol. 48r).

**Page 67.** *Beginning Construction of the Monastery of Bern in 1420,* detail of a miniature in Diebold Schilling, *Chronique priviez de Berne, dit de Spiez* (*The Private Chronicle of Bern, As Told by Spiez*), mid-15th century, Bern, Bürgerbibliothek (MS. hist. helv. I, 1, fol. 451).

# Bibliography

Bechmann, Roland. *Villard de Honnecourt, la pensée technique au XIIIe siècle.* Paris: Picard, 1991.

——. *Les Racines des cathédrales.* Paris: Payot, 1996.

Bowie, Theodore, ed. *The Sketchbook of Villard de Honnecourt.* Westport, Conn.: Greenwood, 1982.

Branner, Robert. *Chartres Cathedral.* New York: Norton, 1969.

Braunstein, Philippe. "Grands Chantiers et hommes de l'art," in *Cahiers de sciences et vie* (Aug. 1996).

Brissac, Catherine. *Le Vitrail.* Paris: Editions de La Martinière, 1994.

Burckhardt, Titus. *Chartres et la naissance de la cathédrale.* Paris: Arché/La Nef de Salomon, 1995.

*Carnet de Villard de Honnecourt, 13ème siècle.* Paris: Stock, 1986.

*Chantiers médiévaux.* Paris: Editions du Zodiaque, 1996.

Clifton-Taylor, Alec. *The Cathedrals of England.* London: Thames and Hudon, 1986.

Coldstream, Nicola. *Masons and Sculptors.* London: British Museum Press, 1991.

Delaissé, L.M.J. *Medieval Miniatures.* New York: Harry N. Abrams, 1965.

Dez, René. *Regius, manuscrit 1390, première lueur de l'aube au pied des cathédrales, la charte la plus ancienne des franc-mestiers de*

*bâtisseurs.* Paris: Librairie du compagnonnage, 1987.

du Colombier, Pierre. *Les Chantiers des cathédrales.* Paris: Picard, 1973.

Erlande-Brandenburg, Alain. *Cathedrals and Castles: Building in the Middle Ages.* New York: Harry N. Abrams, 1995.

——. *Notre-Dame de Paris.* New York: Harry N. Abrams, 1998.

Evans, Joan, ed. *The Flowering of the Middle Ages.* New York: McGraw-Hill, 1966.

Favier, Jean. *The World of Chartres.* New York, Harry N. Abrams, 1990.

Fitchen, John. *The Construction of Gothic Cathedrals.* Oxford: Clarendon, 1961.

Gimpel, Jean. *The Cathedral Builders.* New York: HarperCollins, 1983.

Grodecki, Louis. *Gothic Architecture.* New York: Harry N. Abrams, 1985.

Harvey, John Hooper. *The Medieval Architect.* New York: St. Martin's, 1972.

Icher, François. *La France des compagnons.* Paris: Editions de La Martinière, 1994.

Knoop, Douglas, and G. P. Jones. *The Medieval Mason.* New York: Barnes and Noble, 1967.

Macaulay, David. *Cathedral: The Story of Its Construction.* Boston: Houghton Mifflin, 1973.

MacDonald, Fiona. *A Medieval Cathedral.* New York: P. Bedrick Books, 1994.

Merlin, Peter. *Les Plus Belles Cathédrales.* Verlagsgesellschaft, 1991.

Mortet, Victor, and Paul Deschamps. *Recueil de textes relatifs à l'histoire de l'architecture.* Paris: Editions Auguste Ricard, 1929.

Murray, Stephen. *Building Troyes Cathedral.* Bloomington: Indiana University Press, 1987.

Nefontaine, Luc. *La Franc-maçonnerie, une fraternité dévoilée.* Paris: Gallimard, 1994.

Norman, Edward R. *The House of God: Church Architecture, Style, and History.* New York: Thames and Hudson, 1990.

Perdrizet, Marie-Pierre, and Eddy Krähenbühl. *The Cathedral Builders.* Milbrook Press, 1992.

Petzold, Andreas. *Romanesque Art.* New York: Harry N. Abrams, 1995.

Schock-Werner, Barbara. "Le Chantier de la cathédrale de Strasbourg," in *Chantiers médiévaux.* Editions du Zodiaque, DDB, 1995.

Snyder, James. *Medieval Art: Painting, Sculpture, Architecture, 4th–14th Century.* New York: Harry N. Abrams, 1989.

Verguez, Raoul. *Les Tours inachevées.* Julliard, 1959.

Wilson, Christopher. *The Gothic Cathedral: The Architecture of the Great Church, 1130–1530.* London: Thames and Hudson, 1990.

Zehnacker, Michael. *La Cathédrale de Strasbourg.* Paris: Robert Laffont, 1993.

# Index

# Photograph Credits

For pages with multiple images, the page numbers are labeled a, b, c, according to the picture's position on the page, going clockwise from the upper left.

**Amiens:** Inventaire Général de Picardie, 28.
**Bern:** Bürgerbibliothek, 67, 74b.
**Bourges:** F. Thomas: 96, 97, 105a, 115b, 130–31.
**Brussels:** Bibliothèque Royale Albert Ier, 80, 162; Musée municipal, 89.
**Chartres:** E. Fiévet, 188.
**Dublin:** Trinity College Library, 57.
**London:** British Library, 87b, 166; J. F. Kersting, 8, 25, 113, 116–17.
**Mâcon:** G. Petit/Ville de Mâcon, 101a.
**Nüremberg:** Germanisches Nationalmuseum, 68.
**Paris:** AKG Photo, 10a and b, 17, 35a, 62, 71, 81, 86, 94, 122–23, 127a; All rights reserved, 164; Artephot/J.-P. Dumontier, 42; Artephot/A. Held, 83; B.N.F., 14, 20, 22–23, 39b, 52, 63, 79b, 127b, 145, 146, 147, 148, 149, 155b; Coll. Banque de France. 40a, 41b and c; Bulloz, 16, 66, 100; C.N.M H.S./Archives photographiques, 114; J.-L. Charmet, 29, 156, 160, 161, 185; S. Chirol, 36–37, 43, 51, 129, 133a and b, 136, 138–39; Compagnons du devoir, 157; Créacom, 74a and c, 79a, 101b, 105b, 118a and b; Dagli Orti, 103, 168; Edimedia, 21, 22a, 53, 64; M. Garanger, 98; Giraudon: 11b, 46, 47, 92, 99, 102, 104, 132, 142b, 143, 158–59; Alinari-Giraudon, 18–19; Art Ressource-Giraudon, 177; Bridgeman-Giraudon, 7, 11a, 34, 120, 121, 124a, 141, 170, 179, 182; Lauros-Giraudon, 41a, 69, 154, 170, 175, 187; Hoa-Qui/W. Buss, 99b; Hoa-Qui/S. Grandadam, 99a; The Image Bank/A. Pistolesi, 26–27; H. Josse, 40b, 44, 45; R.M.N./R. G. Ojeda, 14–15; Rapho/R. & S. Michaud, 115a; Roger-Viollet, 119, 140, 142a, 155a; J.-F. Rollinger, endsheets, 30, 70, 76–77, 90–91, 106, 125, 126, 128, 135, 152–53, 172–73; Selva, 13, 84, 85, 93, 95, 110–11, 112, 124b, 167.
**Regensburg (Ratisbon):** Museum der Stadt Regensburg, 54.
**Reims:** Inventaire général, 65.
**Strasbourg:** Archives municipales/E. Laemmel, 50, 58; Bibliothèque nationale et universitaire, 56a; Musées de Strasbourg, 59, 60–61, 144, 150–51, 151; F. Zvardon, 88, 150.
**Toulouse:** S.T.C./Mairie de Toulouse, 33.
**Troyes:** Maison de l'Outil et de la Pensée Ouvrière, 56b.
**Vanves:** Explorer: A. Autenzio, 82; J.-L. Bohin, 108–9; J. Damase, 75; B. Gérard, 134; S. Grandadam, 31; J.-M. Labat, 12, 32, 38a and b, 137, 180–81; A. Le Toquin, 35b, 48–49, 55; Mary Evans Picture Library, 87a; A. Philippon, 39a; Sitko, 107; P. Weisbecker, 78.
**Vienna:** Österreichische Nationalbibliothek, Bildarchiv, 72–73.

Library of Congress Cataloging-in-Publication Data
Icher, François.
[Les œuvriers des cathédrales. English]
Building the great cathedrals / François Icher ;
translated from the French by Anthony Zielonka.
p. cm.
Includes bibliographical references and index.
ISBN 0-8109-4017-5 (hardcover)
1. Cathedrals—History. I. Title.
NA4830.I2713 1998
726.6'094'0902—dc21 98-25867

Printed and bound in Italy

Harry N. Abrams, Inc.
100 Fifth Avenue
New York, N.Y. 10011
www.abramsbooks.com